BADASS LAWMAN

Gangs, Guns and the Sheriff Who Tamed
The Golden State

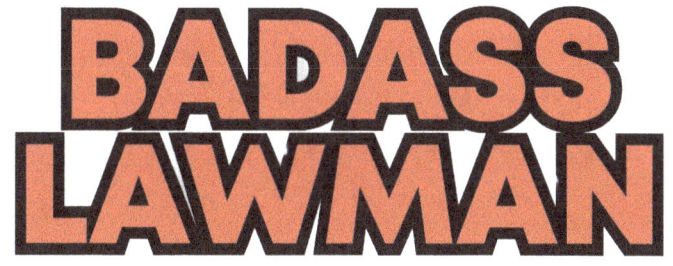

Gangs, Guns and the Sheriff Who Tamed The Golden State

William Briggs

Published by
William Briggs
Morgan Hill, CA 95037
4924_3

ISBN 978-1-956785-23-4

Table of Contents

Foreword

In my role as a professor of criminal justice at Missouri Baptist University, I've tracked the evolution of law enforcement as the United States expanded in the 19th century, including from roots such as Edwardsville, Illinois where this story takes its start. As a Midwesterner, I'm proud of the role our region played as the "Gateway to the West". So, I was drawn to this work about a young man from Illinois who became a famous gunfighter lawman in California. Here in *Badass Lawman,* Dr. William Briggs illuminates the dynamism of America in the 1800s, refracted through the prism of one noble American's life.

Uncovering the forgotten significance of Sheriff John Hicks Adams's life and career, Briggs offers a vivid, well-written account of society, culture and crime on the nineteenth century frontier. With a honed talent for historical storytelling, he takes the reader on a cross country journey with Sheriff Adams, illuminating migration patterns and ever-changing mores in antebellum America.

Badass Lawman explains Sheriff Adams's growth and decision making as he navigates from western Illinois to the Pacific Coast, allowing us to see clearly the movement of our country and its principles, judgements and actions. We see how Adams was affected by his stance within the abolitionist movement, Mexican War service, thirst for wealth in the California Gold Rush, turmoil during the American Civil War, love, family, community activism and as a sheriff in an unstable environment.

John Hicks Adams first entered law enforcement as deputy sheriff to his father in Edwardsville, Illinois. By the end of his career, he had been elected sheriff in Santa Clara County, California five times. He battled the worst willful transgressions of criminal action California could present: lust, sex, bias, murder, theft and robbery, and was still policing this depraved environment as a deputy U.S. Marshal when he was killed in the line of duty. Through Adams's life, we see the full spectrum of exemplary character, allegiance to country and a willingness to enforce the laws which govern society.

In books I recommend, I expect the reader to leave more informed and challenged as to their own next steps in life. As an Americanist who focuses my own research on crime in American society, I deem this piece of well-researched historical storytelling a trifecta: allegorical, informative and thought provoking.

Loftin C. Woodiel, Ph.D.
Rosewood Heights, Illinois

Preface

The genesis of this story is literally rooted in the land. My daughter and her husband had purchased a home set in a vineyard. Among the grapes were some old-vine, head pruned Carignane plantings. This ancient Spanish varietal is uncommon in California, and I wondered who had planted it. Having pursued my own family history in depth, I thought, "why not do the genealogy of a property?"

The property had once been part of a Mexican land grant, and with a little research I discovered the owner of this land after the California gold rush had been a Santa Clara County sheriff named John Hicks Adams. I did a little more research. Adams didn't plant the vines – that happened later – but I was hooked, nevertheless. This 19th century lawman piqued my curiosity. With such a history, why wasn't Adams better known?

I found a few references to Adams online and a couple articles in magazines aimed at an "old west" readership. I even found him listed among the great gunfighter-lawmen in history, along with luminaries such as "**W**ild Bill" Hickok, Seth Bullock, Bat Masterson and Wyatt Earp.

If so, where were the books, the television and film dramatizations, the public popularity of this true western hero?

I have always embraced history. My childhood heroes were often cowboys. I was mesmerized by the radio serials of Roy and Gene and Hoppy and by the early western film stars. I was as caught up in the Disney-Davy Crockett craze as any other kid in 1950's America. History was my favorite subject in school, my favorite genre of literature, my chosen form of escape entertainment. Anything costumed in a Roman toga, medieval armor, as a pirate or in pioneer buckskin held my interest. Declaring as a history major for my baccalaureate at Stanford was an easy decision. As a journalist I always sought the background. As an academic, I became the departmental default professor of American Media History and Historical Method for nearly three decades. In retirement I took on co-presidency of the local historical society. The opportunity to tell this story seemed like a gift.

I have also always self-identified as a Californian. Even abroad, such an introduction has always elicited a smile of recognition: surfer dudes on SoCal beaches, hippies in the Haight during the Summer of Love, convertibles cruising through Napa Valley vineyards, palm trees and redwoods, high-tech billionaires. California has always seemed unique compared to the rest of the country. Not out of step but rather a step ahead on social movements or popular culture. Here we turned waitresses or lifeguards into movie stars and movie stars into governors and a president. We built our own world-class universities and paved freeways to everywhere. And California history was unique too. On this side of the Sierra Nevada, we built models of the Spanish missions in fourth grade and drew murals of gold miners. We took field trips to the old capital at Monterey and Sutter's Fort. We identified with the writings of Mark Twain, Bret Harte, John Steinbeck and Wallace Stegner. We took all the Spanish names of people and places for granted. San Francisco was simply "The City" but never "Frisco."

But telling this story of John Hicks Adams is not an exercise in reliving childhood fantasy. It is a work of historical journalism, written without an agenda other than to tell a good story well and in some detail. It is the story of a big slice of American history, viewed through the prism of a single heroic individual. His story illustrates some events and themes that may have been neglected or glossed over in school. It is a history that also touches on some unpleasant-and perhaps uncomfortable facts. Drawn from contemporary sources, personal journals, family recollections and diverse secondary sources, it is ultimately a tale I hope readers will enjoy and from which take away a better appreciation for a time that was.

Early on I decided not to dramatize Adams's life or invent a lot of dialogue. Of the few instances where I recreated a scene, it was solely for the purpose of moving the narrative along and drawn from the best evidence available. Any excesses of creativity are my responsibility alone.

During the early weeks of my research, I was learning about J.H. Adams's boyhood in Edwardsville, Illinois. On October 10, 2021, a violent tornado ripped through several states and tore the roof from a large distribution warehouse in Edwardsville, killing half a dozen workers inside. Edwardsville was displayed on the front page and the lead story on the evening news. Suddenly, this Californian felt a kinship with the people of Edwardsville. This work is dedicated to the memory of those victims.

William Briggs
Morgan Hill, California
2022

Introduction

"From the beginning, American California was caught in a paradox of reverent awe and exploitative use."

–Kevin Starr, *California: A History*

March 19, 1875. It was a hanging day in San Jose, California. Tiburcio Vasquez, California's most wanted killer and bandit, was about to pay for his nearly two decades of crime. The man in charge of the grim proceedings was Santa Clara County Sheriff John Hicks Adams. The execution of this notorious *bandido* would solidify Sheriff Adams's reputation as one of the top law enforcement officers in the young state of California. Busy officiating at the execution at hand, he probably didn't reflect on how far a journey he had made from his Illinois roots.

In the early decades of the 19th century, the American west still lied east of the Mississippi River. Then followed a series of enormous land acquisitions-the Louisiana Purchase (1803), Texas annexation (1845), the Treaty of Guadalupe Hidalgo (1848) and the Gadsden Purchase (1853). By midcentury the United States had gained the entire middle swath of North America. Land, fortune and opportunity lured Americans westward.

At first only a few explorers and fur trappers ventured across the continent. Soon, however, missionaries and small numbers of other brave settlers in covered wagons had forged the Oregon Trail. Mormons had pushed their handcarts across the plains to establish their community in the Valley of the Great Salt Lake. Then Gold was discovered in California, triggering the migration of hundreds of thousands of pioneers all the way to the Pacific coast as indigenous native Americans looked on with foreboding.

This is the story of one of those individuals, John Hicks Adams. He was an ordinary man who lived an extraordinary life. Born to a modest family in a modest western Illinois town, J.H. Adams would in sequence become a soldier, Indian fighter, wagon master, gold miner, rancher, politician, county sheriff, deputy U.S. marshal, and martyred hero. He would settle and raise a family in the newly created State of California. And he would earn a legacy as one of the premier gunfighter lawmen of the old west.

The story of J.H. Adams is full of drama; he packed more miles on the trail, hostile encounters, danger, hardship, courage, popular acclaim and luck into his life than most would imagine possible. As an officer in the Mexican War, he wore the rank of command comfortably. In the rugged, violent life of the gold camps, he scratched out enough of the yellow metal to establish his family in California. As sheriff, J.H. Adams faced down some of the most notorious, vicious outlaws of his day and emerged from the gun smoke unscathed. His reputation as a lawman earned him a contemporary record five terms as Sheriff in Santa Clara County. In an era when law enforcement often meant staying one step in front of an angry lynch mob, Sheriff Adams made sure those he arrested received fair trial and the justice they deserved.

But in a larger sense, this is more than a singular, exciting story of one man's life, it is also a tale embossed on a panoramic canvass of American history, including less familiar episodes such as California's unique role in the Civil War, how the speed of communication depended upon the mode of transportation, or the importance of quicksilver during the gold rush. We cannot read of J.H. Adams without vicariously following the wagons west, crossing the plains, desert and high mountain passes. His life takes us to old civilizations on the plains, the southwest and in California, where, in the words of Samuel P. Huntington, civilizations clashed. Pawnee, Zuni, Amah Mutsun and *Californio* peoples all encountered the relentless surge of American westward expansion in search of

God or gold or land. And just as J.H. Adams played his part in the so-called Manifest Destiny of the country, he also was caught up in the internal culture clashes within his own society as it wrestled with deep divisions over slavery, states' rights, land ownership, and the imposition of U.S. authority over the former Mexican territory of Alta California. As a county sheriff during the Civil War, which deeply divided California despite its distance from the eastern battlefields, J.H. Adams remained loyal to the republic and played a major role in ridding California of any serious secessionist threats. As a peacekeeper in a lawless environment, he faced challenges beyond the control of a single individual, but by the time he died at the relatively early age of 58, he had helped move the needle in California law enforcement toward public safety and prosperity for all.

At the appointed hour, Sheriff Adams sent Vasquez dropping through the gallows floor. The huge crowd gasped at the climactic end to this chapter of crime and punishment in early California history. More chapters would yet follow for the resolute lawman, but this story begins in western Illinois, not far from the Mississippi River...

Chapter 1

Edwardsville, Illinois

"The business of the Mississippi, which it will accomplish in time, is methodically to transport all of Illinois to the Gulf of Mexico."

–Charles Kuralt, CBS News

In 1820, The West, for the few hundred hardy residents of Edwardsville, Illinois, extended only a few miles farther in that direction and stopped at the sandy banks of the great Mississippi River. Beyond that, across the surface of the broad silting and swirling current, and above the stout grass that reached taller than a man and clung to the bluffs of the flood plain, lay the vast, unobstructed line of sight of the North American prairie. This world beyond Madison County was still virtually unknown and unexplored. Indian Country. *Terra incognita.*

The land which stretched beyond the horizon into the setting sun was not totally unknown, however. For years Mountain Men, trappers in greasy buckskins, accompanied by

5

their Native American wives and mixed-race children, would occasionally return to civilization along the Missouri or Mississippi Rivers with tall stacks of fur pelts and even taller tales. In 1814, the publication of *The History of the Expedition Under Commands of Captains Lewis and Clark* had enjoyed a modest reception. Drawn from the journals of Meriwether Lewis, the book described the 1803-1806 expedition by the Corps of Discovery across the Louisiana Purchase to the Pacific coast of Oregon. But as Lewis's biographer Stephen Ambrose observed, "Lewis's glowing reports on the soil and climate in present Missouri, Kansas, Iowa, and Nebraska had not set off a land rush; there was still plenty of land to be had in Kentucky, Illinois, Indiana, Ohio."[1] As for California, that land farthest west was almost a total mystery, although it had long captured the public's imagination as a land of great bounty and riches; possibly even an island inhabited by giant women warriors. Within a generation, this world view and this nation would be dramatically and permanently altered.

Illinois, itself, was still a largely unsettled frontier. Originally claimed for France by the explorers Marquette and Jolliet in the 17th century, *La Louisiane* had been ceded to the British at the conclusion of the Seven Years War (known in America as the French & Indian War). During the American War for Independence, colonial Ranger George Rogers Clark (older brother of explorer William Clark) had wrested the territory from British-backed hostile natives before it became part of Indiana Territory in the new United States of America. Among the first settlers along the Goshen Trail on the western fringe of the territory was Ninian Edwards, for whom Edwardsville township was named. In short order Illinois became a territory of its own and achieved statehood by 1818. Ninian Edwards became the new state's first governor. (In all, Edwardsville would see five of its native sons become governors of Illinois).[2]

About 1818 , a young couple made their way from New York down the Ohio River to Shawneetown, then over the Goshen Trail to Edwardsville. The husband, John Quincy Adams, was not of strong constitution and had sought out less strenuous alternatives than farming for making a living. He had apprenticed as a fuller (wool processor) and had shipped a pair of wool "pulling" (carding) machines ahead to St. Louis where he sold one mill. He set up the other mill in Edwardsville. Adams, (not to be confused with the U.S. presidents of the same name, may have been a very distant cousin of the same Massachusetts political dynasty that produced a pair of presidents. However, according to Magnus Ryrie Milner, Adams's 2X great grandson who transcribed Adams's handwritten Journal, there was no family tie). [3] John Quincy

7

had been born in Vermont in 1796 to Revolutionary War veteran Jonathon Matthews "Capt." Adams of Connecticut and Sarah "Sally" Daniels of Vermont. His wife of two years, Hannah Anne Hicks, was born in 1799, in Cayuga, New York. Her parents were Jacob Hicks and Mary (Polly) Hand. Upon settling in Edwardsville, together they would add seven children to the community between 1819 and 1833. Their first son, John Hicks Adams, joined the family in 1820, followed by William and Harriet. Called J.H. to differentiate himself from his father, he was destined to live a life no one would have envisioned, in places no one had even imagined. And he would become a legend.

Basic survival needs of his family would have been John Quincy's top priority. Their first rough- hewn log cabin with a pitched roof to repel winter snows would have been a simple one room design with a door, single window and stone hearth for cooking and warmth. Furniture was simply a plank table and benches and wooden platform beds with straw filled mattresses suspended over hemp rope lattice, in which the children slept heads to feet. Coverings were rough woolen blankets and wool clothing dressed them all since John Quincy Adams was a fuller by trade - someone who cleans and thickens wool prior to making it into cloth. Later the home was remodeled using hand-sawed lumber from the surrounding oak and hickory forest. As the family prospered, John Quincy would eventually erect a two-story brick residence on the west side of City Park Square on South Kansas Street.[4]

Feeding the population was a never-ending effort. Slowly the native grasslands gave way to fenced-in farmland. One early settler noted the roots of the grass were so tough to break up with his cast iron plow and wooden mouldboard that it required three yoke of oxen or six horses. But after one year, he added, "the ground is mellow and requires but a light team to plow it." [5] Within a few years this mellow ground of Madison County was producing market fruit and vegetables, as well as winter wheat, corn, rye and barley for flour, brewing beer and making whiskey. (A short distance from the north end of town on the banks of the Cahokia Creek stood the Klingel Brewery. Caves in the hillside naturally cooled the fermenting beer. Nearby the distillery received wagon loads of corn from local farmers. By the 1830s Edwardsville provided a pair of public houses for thirsty residents. Big city competition and railroad distribution would eventually put the local brewery and distillery out of business.). In those early days, domestic livestock grazed freely in the grassy cleared fields. Horses and oxen did the heavy work; dairy cattle, poultry and hogs all contributed protein to the local diet. We know that lamb was available as well; John Quincy had erected a fulling mill on the

Chahokia Creek and was using a carding machine of his own design at the corner of Main and Vandalia to disentangle, clean and combine the sheep's wool fibers. He later sold the business to partner George W. Putnam. [6]

In his Journal, Adams wrote, [I] *built a pulling Mill on Cahokia creek which cost about two hundred dollars but whether being extremely dry I did not have water surfishent to pull until the ensuing March. {sic}* [7]

The natural environment around Edwardsville also supplied the townsfolk with food. Elderberries, wild plums and other fruit grew in profusion under the canopy of oaks and walnut trees. The buffalo herds that had roamed Illinois since the end of the last glacial epoch had all migrated west into those unknown prairies, followed by most of the indigenous natives that had lived with the herds and had depended upon them for thousands of years. But a few elk and bear remained in the vicinity. Small game and fowl were common meal additions, as were fish from free-running streams. J.H. Adams would have learned about hunting from early boyhood and become familiar with firearms, particularly the Kentucky long rifles whose twisting grooves along its interior bore increased its accuracy and could be better aimed by the hunter than the faster loading smooth bore musket favored by the military. America had been conceived and birthed in a fog of gunpowder. Many local men had been veterans of the Revolution, the War of 1812 or the Black Hawk Indian War. Every family had a weapon for defense and hunting. J.H. Adams would not only become experienced with a wide variety of 19th century firearms but would develop such expertise as a soldier and peace officer that the sobriquet *pistolero* would become part of his legacy.

When he was territorial governor in 1809, Ninian Edwards had used the cabin of Edwardsville founder Thomas Kirkpatrick along Cahokia Creek as the first seat of justice for Madison County. Another log structure served as the courthouse and anchored the town's first public square on North Main Street. Later local businessmen would replace it with a two-story brick courthouse.[8] An adjacent log cabin served as the county jail, which would figure into the life of the Adams family *pere et fils.* In addition, when J.H. Adams was born, the town already had more than 60 houses, a public bank, printing office, U.S. Land Office, and a Methodist Church. John Quincy Adams was a prominent member of the Baptist congregation and helped erect a church in 1828. A printing office at what became Main and Lincoln streets, housed the first newspaper, *The Spectator*, owned by Hooper Warren. For a while *The Spectator* was the most widely read newspaper in the state before it folded in 1826.[9]

Other early citizens included Benjamin Stephenson, a pro-slavery Virginian who served as delegate to congress from the Illinois Territory in 1814, and Dr. John Todd, a Kentucky physician who was also uncle to both the wife of Ninian Edwards and the wife of Abraham Lincoln, Mary Todd. John T. Lusk, a veteran Ranger of the War of 1812, helped build a defensive fort on the outskirts of town to protect from any Indian raids, and left his wife, a crack markswoman, in charge of the women who took refuge in the fort during the Black Hawk War while the men were away. Lusk later built the first hotels in Edwardsville. General James D. Henry had the distinction of capturing Chief Black Hawk to end that war.[10]

Between 1825 and 1830, Illinois population swelled from 75,000 to 161,000 inhabitants. In 1831, J. M. Peck wrote *Guide for Emigrants, containing sketches of Illinois, Missouri and the Adjacent Parts*, extolling the advantages of Madison County: "Goshen, Marine, Woodriver, Gilham's and Ridgeprairie are all fine and flourishing settlements of industrious farmers, its towns are Alton (upper and lower), Edwardsville and Collinsville." [9.] By 1833, Edwardsville had a population of 350.[11]

Young J.H. Adams probably attended school in the wood framed building next to the jail, taught by John York Sawyer before he left to edit the newspaper. Those frontier schools were called *loud schools*, as the students recited their lesson out loud. A succession of teachers followed, and class was often held in private homes. After 1830 a learned instructor named John Barber taught school three miles south of town. John Quincy Adams was influential in the establishment of the Edwards Female Academy in 1831, which suffered from faculty turnover, as the female teachers peeled off to get married.[12] As the oldest son, J.H. shouldered much of the responsibility of helping with the family enterprises. Yet his education was also deemed important. His mother, Hannah Hicks Adams, took ill and died April 30,1833 at the young age of 33. John Q. Adams wrote, *"[My wife] continued to decline and that her disease was becoming a Settled consumption...a part of March and all of Aprill she was confined to her bed. She retained her sences until the last perfectly---the last day of April it pleased her heavenly father to take her from this world of pain and trouble"*.[13.] After his mother's death, his father sent J.H. off to board at Alton College and Seminary (later Shurtleff College) in Upper Alton. He would remain there two years.

Founded in 1827 as Rock Springs Seminary, the school moved to Alton in 1832 and offered both liberal arts and theology curricula under the leadership of Rev. Hubbel Loomis, principal from 1832 – 1835. Private schools of the day commonly included an academy for high school age students.

13

J.H. Adams and a few dozen of his peers followed a traditional course of study, but also were exposed to music and household arts, along with the older college students. After J.H. left, the school was renamed Shurtleff College, recognizing a major donor and in 1957 it was folded into Southern Illinois University.[14]

In order to provide a mother for his children, widower John Quincy Adams had remarried while J.H. was away at school. *"I at length became acquainted with Miss Rebecca Gordon of Carlton (aged about 29 years) and believed in her I had found the person desired as one of hevens gifts to fill the important Station in my affections and family as wife to my Self and mother to my children...my children were well pleased with their new mother."* [15.] Together they would have three more children.

Returning from boarding school, J.H. Adams was a welcome addition to the family labor force. In addition to manufacturing woolen goods, John Quincy Adams was a serious entrepreneur. Since 1822, he had been engaged in the production of castor oil, the first such mill in the state. While modern society may think of castor oil as a foul -tasting laxative, it has been used for a wide variety of cosmetic, medicinal and other uses since the days of the pharaohs. In pre-industrial, pre-petroleum America, castor oil was an important

14

machine lubricant and illuminated the lamps of frontier cabins and businesses. An article in the *Jacksonville [Illinois] Journal* claimed "Castor oil is better for lamps than sperm or lard oil, which is the fact. Some years since, when this oil was cheaper than either of the others, the editors of that paper used it in their parlor lamps, much pleased with the result; it is a white, clear, beautiful light, and does not clog the wick."[16] Nineteenth century peddlers often cut the castor oil with liberal amounts of grain spirits and sold the alcoholic snake oil as a cure for a wide variety of ills from baldness to labor pains in pregnancy. This cure may have been worse than the ailment.

(Castor oil may yet prove to be a significant renewable biodiesel energy source, however labor and other economic factors have inhibited its development in the U.S.)

John Adams wrote of his business in his Journal: *My carding business this year 1825 amounted to almost the same as the year before, I built an oil press that fall which was attended with considerable difficulty not being well aquainted with the business I purchased a vary large iron screw and hed an ironplate follower and tubs made and after making alterations and repairs I sucseded in getting it in operation after expending about three hundred dollars I purchased about four hundred bushels of Castor beans that fall of which I made about seven hundred gallan of oil. I sent two hundred and fifty*

15

gallons to New York which sold for one dollar twelve and half cents per gallon the rest I traded different places from one dollar fifty cents to two dollars per gallon."[17]

Back in Edwardsville, J.H. rolled up his sleeves and worked with his siblings and father in the castor oil business. John Quincy had obtained a small quantity of castor seeds (*Ricinus communis* L.) and shared them with neighbors who planted them. Native to Eastern Africa and India, the fast-growing shrub adapted to the well-drained soil and climate of the Mississippi Basin and unfortunately soon spread as an invasive species, although for the Adams's venture supply seemed to match demand. At harvest, J.H. and the others picked the spiny green capsules containing the large oval castor beans by hand. It was laborious and draining work in the humidity of southern Illinois. His father paid a dollar a bushel for the beans.

Manufacture of castor oil was as labor intensive as the harvest. After removing the hulls from the seeds by hand, the beans were allowed to dry in the warmth of the sun. The seeds were then roasted, ground in a cold press (most likely designed by John Quincy himself) and the paste boiled, allowing the oil to be scooped from the top after cooling, leaving the toxin ricin behind. To remove impurities, which caused rapid degradation of the oil, the process could be repeated.[18.] Demand for the popular lubricant grew and the Adams family prospered until 1838 when disaster struck. *"[I] had made near thirty barrels of oil when early on the morning of the 11th of May 1838 the mill was consumed by fire with what beans I had on hand about 1500 bushels and ten or twelve barrels of oil besides considerable other property I had in the mill the whole loss was about five thousand dollars---As I had a quantity of the beans bot of Mecker and the iron presses not much injoured I concluded to put up a tempory building and continue the business---Putnam again rented the machine and John H worked with him to be enable to carry it on himself.* "19. The uninsured loss probably would be valued at ten times as great in today's dollars. Undaunted, John Quincy rebuilt but shifted much of the operation to his sons, as he also took on public service. He continued operating the factory until his death in 1840 J.H. continued the business for two more years with a partner, his wife's brother-in-law Henry King Eaton.20

The Eaton family had originally traveled up the Mississippi River from New Orleans and settled on a large government land grant in Madison County. Drawn to public service, in 1839 Henry King Eaton was elected justice of the peace. After helping J.H. Adams with the castor oil business for a while, he devoted himself full-time to his public duties. In 1842 he became a deputy sheriff, followed by stints as revenue commissioner and census commissioner. He served as probate judge of Madison County from 1846 to 1850, and was elected Madison County Judge, retiring in 1857 after overseeing the disposition of the estate of Elijah P. Lovejoy, a minister and fierce abolitionist publisher whose death helped spark the Civil War.[21].

Lovejoy had been hounded out of St. Louis and removed to Alton where he began printing the *Alton Observer* and was an active member of the local Anti-Slavery Society, continuing to publish anti-slavery columns. Angry pro-slavery mobs destroyed Lovejoy's printing presses three times, throwing them into the Mississippi. When a fourth press arrived on November 7, 1837, an angry mob attacked the warehouse where it was stored, first with rocks, then bullets, then fire. Lovejoy was killed and left in the burning building. No one was ever convicted of the murder. Lovejoy became a martyred hero to both the abolitionist cause and to freedom of the press. Events shape public opinion. The death shocked the nation and intensified the polarization over slavery in the border states of Illinois and Missouri, foreshadowing violence to come. Perhaps with only minor exaggeration, it has been said that the Lovejoy murder, along with John Brown's raid on Harper's Ferry, were the two events which most hastened the American Civil War. [22]

Although the Adams family did not own slaves, it would have been impossible to avoid forming opinions about the greatest issue of 19th Century America, what Pulitzer Prize-winning writer Nikole Hannah-Jones calls "America's original Sin."[23]. The Northwest Ordinance of 1787 prohibited slavery in land ceded to the Federal government. However, Southern Illinois had been largely settled by southerners from slave states, and several had brought their enslaved human chattel with them. The Territorial Legislature, and later the new Illinois State Legislature called for transfer from slave to indentured servant status, a hugely flawed compromise which changed little. So-Called "Black Codes", making indentured African Americans second-class citizens remained in effect until after the Civil War. Madison County had been a crucial battleground in an early effort to hold a constitutional convention to make Illinois a slave state in 1824, an effort ultimately defeated by the voters by a margin of 14 percent.[24.] For the next couple decades, the cauldron of controversy over slavery intensified from simmer to boil. Witnessing these early battles over slavery would affect J.H. for life. He would move west and face racial interaction and government policies regarding Hispanics, Native Americans and Chinese as well as African Americans. As a public servant officer of the law, J.H. Adams would be sworn enforce the laws regarding the issue of race. By the time the cauldron boiled over decades later into terrifying civil war at Ft. Sumpter, J.H. would be two thousand miles away In California, where the blue-grey clash of arms over slavery would unfold much differently.

Meanwhile, J.H. Adams operated the castor oil business with his brother William Robert, until a sharp drop in market prices forced suspension in 1842. Market fluctuation, however, didn't discourage everyone from producing the oil. In the neighboring community of Alton, the *Alton Telegraph* reported that Marsh, Hankinson & Co., Druggists commenced manufacturing castor oil in November 1841: "This will afford farmers in the vicinity a cash market for another article of their product easily raised – the Castor Bean." [25.] By then, J.H. Adams was ready to write new chapters in his life.

Both John Quincy and J.H. Adams no doubt benefitted from their familial ties to Henry King Eaton and were influenced by his role in public service. John Quincy developed his own sense of public service and wrote in his diary: *"After my oil mill was burnt I was persuaded to become a candidate for the office of Sheriff and on the 1st Monday of August 1838 was elected to fill that Station."* [26.] (The position of sheriff traces far back to Anglo Saxon Britain. Following the Norman Conquest of 1066, England centralized into administrative counties or shires. The *shire reeve* served as local representative of the king with primary responsibility for tax collection. The position of county sheriff migrated to North America with the early English colonists).

As sheriff, John Quincy appointed his son, J.H., to serve as his deputy. This was to prove a life-defining moment for the young man. He was assigned collection of taxes and routine court business. Age eighteen and approaching full manhood, J.H. learned the bureaucracy of local government and became well versed in local law enforcement and the justice system. It is quite likely his clerical deputy's duties proved routine and monotonous for the young man ready for more action. When a pair of incarcerated men took advantage of Sheriff Adams's absence to Municipal Court in Alton and broke out of the county jail, Deputy Sheriff J.H. Adams, led a posse himself in hot pursuit. Young Adams and an old trapper named McIntire tracked the escapees down the St. Louis Road. After several days, the escapees were cornered, pistols misfired during a thunderstorm and the prisoners were apprehended after a desperate struggle and returned to custody.[27.] Sheriff John Adams was extremely pleased with his son and during the following year together they made numerous arrests—mostly gamblers from Missouri plying their trade in Illinois.[28] J.H. Adams had distinguished himself in his initiation as a lawman. He would answer that call several times in his career would

21

one day join the pantheon of iconic gunfighter peace officers of the Old West.

Notes:

1. Stephen E. Ambrose, *Undaunted Courage*, New York: Simon & Shuster, 1996, p. 483.

2. "History of Illinois," https://www.history.com>topicas>us-states>illinois, retrieved Nov. 25, 2021.

3. John Adams, *Journal*, transcribed from the original by Magnus R. Milnor, June 1988, collection of Cheryle Cearlock. The original Journal resides in the collection of Southern Illinois University.

4. "Many Old Houses Still Remain," *Edwardsville Intelligencer,* Centennial Edition, 1912.

5. Ellen Nore, "Madison County (1812-2012): Reflecting Illinois and National History," *Illinois Heritage 15*, No. 6 (November 2012): 15-30.

6. Old Landmark Going," *Edwardsville Intelligencer,* Feb. 24, 1921.

7. John Adams, op.cit. p. 40.

8. "History of Edwardsville," https://townsquarepublications.com/regions/midwest/illinois/edwardsville, retrieved November2 8, 2021.

9. "Old Landmark Going," op. cit.

10. "History of Edwardsville," op. cit.

11. J.M. Peck, *Guide for Emigrants, containing sketches of Illinois, Missouri and the Adjacent Parts*, Boston: Lincoln and Edwards, 1831.

12. "The Early History of Edwardsville and Leclaire," https:// madison.illinoisgenweb.org.town-histories, retrieved Nov. 26, 2021.

13. John Adams, op.cit. p. 52.
14. Shurtleff College, https://www.lostcollegfes.com>shurtleff_college.
15. John Adams, op. cit., pp. 56-57.
16. "Lamp Oil from Castor Beans," *Illinois Historical Anecdotes,* Chicago 1940, http://genealogy trails.com>ill>Illinois, retrieved Dec. 12, 2021.
17. John Adams, op. cit., p. 40.
18. Vinay R. Patel, "Castor Oil: Properties, Uses, and Optimization of Processing Parameters in Commercial Production," https://www.nebi.nlm.nih.gov>articles, (PMC 5015816).
19. John Adams, op. cit., p. 60.
20. Eugene T. Sawyer, *History of Santa Clara County California*, Historic Record Co., 1922.
21. "Descendants of Harry Eaton," http://www.djs.org>eatongenealogyreport.
22. "Elijah Parish Lovejoy," https://www.nationalabolitionhalloffameand museum.org, retrieved Nov. 30, 2021.
23. Nikole Hannah-Jones et al., *The 1619 Project–A New Origin Story*, One World Books, 2021.
24. "Slavery in Madison County," "Madison County (1812-2012): Reflecting Illinois and National History," op. cit.
25. *Alton Telegraph*, November 1841.
26. John Adams, op. cit., p. 60.
27. Sawyer, op. cit.

28. "Capt. John H. Adams, a Mexican Veteran and a 49-er – An Adventurous Life," *San Jose Pioneer Press*, 1878.

William Briggs

Chapter 2

To Arms!

"A strong desire pervades this country that a region extending west of our current possessions to the Pacific Ocean should be acquired."

–Senator Lewis Cass, 1847

One Spring day in 1847, John Hicks Adams walked home deep in thought, a copy of the *Edwardsville Intelligenser* under his arm. A large, printed announcement called for six thousand more volunteers to serve in the U.S. Army in the current war against Mexico. The banner headline read "To Arms! To Arms!" [1.] On April 19th, the Secretary of War had called for the additional troops to replace those whose terms of enlistment had been fulfilled. Illinois was to raise another regiment. J.H. Adams was about to answer the bugle call.

The United State Congress declared war against the Republic of Mexico on May 11, 1846, and authorized the president to levy recruitment of fifty thousand volunteers for a one-year enlistment. More than twice the number of young

Illinois men required enthusiastically had responded, forming four regiments. Those regiments had seen action in Mexico and served with distinction before being discharged between May and June 1847. Now the state was asking for more troops, giving those disappointed the first time a chance to go and fight afterall.[2.]

It has been said, *every generation deserves a war of its own,* and the United States had complied ever since the Revolution: The Second War with Britain, 1812-14; the Black Hawk War 1831-32; and now the Mexican War. (Sadly, the trend has continued to the present day). Illinois men were conditioned to military service by the many veterans living among them. General James D. Henry, who had the distinction of capturing Chief Black Hawk to end that war, had been a resident of Edwardsville.[3] Across the state, in Springfield, a young veteran of the Black Hawk War named Abraham Lincoln was launching his political career. Men on the western frontier were welcome in the military for their familiarity with weapons and because their closer proximity to the theater of war saved on transportation costs.[4.] Young, patriotic men saw wartime service as normal and expected. It was a chance to get off the farm, test themselves, have an adventure.

J.H. Adams was certainly a product of his time and place. He likely was among those who regretted missing the first muster of regiments in 1846. Like his father, he had a background in public service. And he was good with guns. But now he had other considerations. J.H. had married in December 1841. His wife, Matilda Jane Pomeroy, was the eighth child of George Pomeroy and Mary (Polly) Monin. The Pomeroys were transplanted from Pennsylvania, where grandfather Thomas Pomeroy had served in the Cumberland County militia during the Revolution. Great grandfather, Irishman George Holmes Pomeroy, had escaped a British impressment gang and fled to the Colonies aboard an American-bound ship around 1730.[5] Matilda was also the sister-in-law of J.H. Adams's business partner H.K. Eaton.

Together, J.H. and Matilda had started their family. The first three of their children: Mary Hannah (1842), John Washington (1844) and Alice Melissa (1846) were born in Edwardsville. In addition, after his father died, J.H. had assumed guardianship of his own three youngest siblings: DeWitt Clinton (1826), Mary Jane (1828) and Frank (1831). Guardians were responsible for managing the inheritance of minor heirs under 14 years old. At age 14, the minor could petition the court to appoint a guardian of the minor's choice. [6]

There was also a business to support all these children. In 1830, John Quincy Adams had opened a merchandise store, hoping to trade farmers merchandise for castor beans. Since

29

the death of his father and the divestiture of his interest in the castor oil factory, J.H. had been proprietor of the general store at Main and Vandalia Streets, the only business of its kind carried on in UpperTown.[7.] J.H. eventually sold this business to H.C. Soheer, probably before leaving Edwardsville for good in the 1850s. We can get an idea of the scope of this business from a small advertisement in the *Edwardsville Madison County Courier* in 1866:

H.C. Soheer
Dealer in Dry Goods, Groceries
Boots and Shoes, Clothing, Hats and Caps,
Hardware, Queensware, Fancy Goods and
Notions, etc. southwest corner of Main and
Van dalia streets, Edwardsville, Ill.[8]

With all these responsibilities weighing upon him, J.H. Adams must have been conflicted during long conversations with Matilda in the parlor by the light of a castor oil lamp. Nearing thirty years old, J.H. was strong, tough and in his prime, but he was also already well-established in his community. In the end, his sense of duty prevailed. He would go and fight.

It had all started a decade earlier with Texas. The region called Texas had been the northernmost part of the Spanish Empire in North America. Sparsely populated and too remote to administer or defend, the viceroys in Mexico City had encouraged immigration from the United States in order create a buffer against raids of hostile Comanches and other plains Indians, as well as encroachment by another foreign power.

More than anything else, Texas attracted settlers because it offered vast tracts of cheap, fertile land, ideal for growing cotton, a crop that demanded a large labor force to meet expanding market demand. Most American settlers, called Texians, migrated from southern states where slavery was legal. Many brought their slaves with them. But after gaining independence from Spain in 1821, Mexico quickly abolished slavery, threatening the Texian economic land bonanza. Repeal of the Mexican Constitution of 1824, which had given northern Texas a large degree of self-rule, set in motion a revolt against Mexican rule. After bloodshed at the Alamo, Goliad and San Jacinto, Texas achieved independence in 1836, followed by U.S. annexation and then statehood in 1845. A year later Congress would declare war against Mexico.[9]

There certainly had been many underlying causes for the Texas Revolution. Texians were culturally and economically tied to the United States. There were those in the U.S. who secretly—or not so secretly—eyed Texas annexation for territorial gain and expansion of slavery. [10] This more recent emphasis on land and slavery has clashed with the long-

31

standing narrative of the Texas origin story of freedom loving Anglos fighting despotic tyranny.[11] Regardless of cause, the Mexicans never forgot the loss of their northern province and the resentment festered well into the 1840s, when greed, politics, and something called Manifest Destiny brought the two nations to war.

Anglo-Americans had persistently settled in the lands south and west of the Louisiana Purchase. An 1845 newspaper editorial called for the "Fulfillment of our Manifest Destiny to overspread the continent allotted by Providence."[12] In little time, Manifest Destiny came to mean occupying and civilizing the entire continent from Atlantic to Pacific.

As Simon Winchester writes, hunger for land ownership had shaped the modern world. *"...there were the Spanish territories of Texas and California – millions upon millions of acres of land that looked at first quite freely available to any white man who wished to settle and prosper. If any native peoples...happened to stand in the way of this God-given right and duty, then they should, said the settlers and speculators, be brusquely swept aside, all in the name of progress and the common good."[13]*

Mexico had refused to recognize Texas independence. The border was never clearly established. Many Americans openly sympathized with U.S. born Texans and pushed for annexation. As his last act in office, President John Tyler had put through a resolution in Congress calling for the annexation of Texas. To avoid further conflict, Texas was fast-tracked into statehood in 1845. Mexico had threatened war and broke off diplomatic relations. Incoming U.S. President James K. Polk had openly campaigned on a platform of expansion and annexation of Texas, Mexican California and the Oregon Territory, also claimed by Britain.

"Great Britain had been discussing with Mexico for months the possibility of buying California. The British previously had offered to support the independence of Texas in return for the abolition of slavery in the area. Even before settling the Oregon question, Polk had moved troops into the disputed [border] territory just north of the Rio Grande River and sent a special envoy, John Slidell, to Mexico. Slidell carried with him a U.S. offer to buy California as well as plenipotentiary powers to settle disputed border claims." [14]

When U.S. offers were rebuffed, skirmishes between the two sides resulted in bloodshed. The U.S. claimed Mexico had invaded Texas soil north of the claimed border that ran along the Rio Grande River (Mexico claimed the border to be 130 miles farther north along the Nueces River). Congress reacted to this aggression with a Declaration of War on May 13, 1846.

Not everyone in Washington D.C. supported the war. Critics claimed President Polk deliberately provoked Mexico into war, calling it "An expansionist power play dictated by an aggressive southern slave owner's intent on acquiring move slave states".[15.] (Texas had become the fifteenth slave state). First term Illinois congressman Abraham Lincoln condemned the war as unconstitutional, though that position proved unpopular at home. With the advent of the telegraph, the Mexican War became history's first war to be reported on daily. In Edwardsville as elsewhere, citizens scanned the newspapers for details of the regiments already there, seeing action at Buena Vista, Vera Cruz and Cerro Gordo. With war support and Illinois enlistments running high, J.H. Adams set aside any political or family misgivings and assisted in raising Company I, Fifth Illinois Volunteers. He was going to war.

The Fifth Regiment of Illinois Volunteers was to muster at Alton, Illinois on June 8, 1847 under the command of Colonel Edward W.B.Newby While general officers in the Army served at the discretion of the president, regimental and company grade officers of volunteers were elected from the ranks. In Edwardsville, Franklin Niles was elected captain, and, probably due to his community standing. J.H. Adams was elected company first lieutenant. (Recruitment in Edwardsville was so successful and the 5th Regiment so oversubscribed that

Illinois Governor Augustus French was able to form a sixth regiment in August 1847, made up of veterans wanting to return to the fray, as well as new recruits anxious to fight the Mexicans). Thus organized, with an enlistment *for the duration of the war* and a pay rate of $15.50 per month, the eighty-plus men of Captain Niles's Company, marched the fifteen miles from Edwardsville to Alton in high spirits[16]

Captain Franklin David Niles marched his company into Alton, just below the confluence of the Mississippi and Missouri Rivers, on June 2. Niles had moved to Edwardsville from Pennsylvania in 1840 and purchased more than thirteen thousand acres of land. He was the same age as J.H. Adams and was already a veteran of the Mexican War, having served earlier under Colonel Alexander Doniphan in New Mexico, in the Second Regiment of Illinois Volunteers. The two men were well-acquainted. In Alton, after a week of issuing uniforms and equipment, Newby's Regiment boarded a steamer bound upstream to Fort Leavenworth on June 14. Mexico was in the opposite direction.

The trip upstream to their destination, Fort Leavenworth, would take about a week. Established in 1827, on the west bank of the Missouri River, the frontier fort was in what was called "Indian Country." It could only be supplied by river.[17] The new recruits standing at the rail of the riverboat, listening

35

to the slap-slap of the giant paddle wheel fighting upstream against the irresistible current going the other way toward New Orleans would have had lots of time to think. Some surely already missed their families. Perhaps a few now had misgivings about enlisting. Great carbonized clouds of smoke from the insatiable furnaces belched from the boat's smokestack and mixed with steam vapor to spoil the summer sky. Fort Leavenworth was the gateway to the endless prairie and the head of the Santa Fe Trail. Any dreams of glory under the guns of Chapultepec Castle in Mexico City with General Winfield Scott, must have seemed swept away in the muddy currents of this river that drained half a continent. Their war in the southwest would be quite different.

Newby's Regiment arrived at Fort Leavenworth in time to celebrate the 4th of July holiday, marching around the parade ground, hearing the post chaplain read the Declaration of Independence and the firing of a salute from the fort's three nine-pounder cannons. Troops then began preparing for their mission: making the long march to Santa Fe, New Mexico Territory, escorting and guarding wagon trains carrying commissary, quartermaster and other supplies. Describing the challenge for Army quartermasters, Alvin P. Stauffer writes, "Under the wretched physical conditions that confronted the armies in Mexico and the Southwest the ordinary difficulties of transportation and supply were intensified...the fighting forces had to carry with them virtually everything they might need on a campaign. For the first time American armies were fighting in rough, thinly settled, semi-desert areas that were almost totally lacking in roads and deep waterways and that furnished little in the way of supplies. Even fuel and forage were often lacking."[18.] As his first set of orders, J.H. Adams was assigned regimental quartermaster, in charge of all the necessary supplies including 120 wagons to carry it all and the necessary livestock for transportation power and food, for the nearly 900-mile trek through hostile Indian territory to Santa Fe, the longest supply line in U.S. military history. [19]

At Fort Leavenworth, the Illinois troops were joined by the Third Missouri Infantry and the Third Missouri Mounted Volunteers. Lieutenant J.H. Adams faced an enormous task equipping more than two thousand soldiers and preparing for the long march to Santa Fe. But within a couple weeks, wagons were loaded, horses shod, and the various companies began to move out. On July 18th, a detail from two companies departed to accompany Lieutenant Christopher (Kit) Carson (the famous frontier scout, temporarily holding a military commission) who was carrying dispatches to Santa Fe and California.[20.] The Illinois regiment left in stages to stagger access to the limited water available. Niles's Company was assigned guarding the large herd of cattle resupplying the garrison at Santa Fe. Few of the soldiers had imagined they would spend the war herding cows, though all agreed an army travels on its stomach.

As an officer, Lieutenant Adams would have been mounted. He was armed with a model 1842 percussion pistol and caliber.52 Hall-North carbine. A three-foot-long Prussian-made heavy saber hung from a shoulder strap attached to his white belt and large brass buckle embossed with "US". In the heat of prairie summer, he wore a buff cotton jacket and trousers instead of his dark blue single-breasted frock coat and sky-blue trousers. For the trail, he may have opted for a forage cap instead of the stove pipe Shako hat. Shoulder straps edged in silver lace indicated his rank, which would change much sooner than anyone expected.[21]

Not long into the march, at a place called 110 Mile Creek (based on distance from the Fort Leavenworth flagpole) Captain Franklin Niles died on July 24, 1847. Though his death was widely reported, there is no mention of cause in either military reports or civilian press coverage. He most likely succumbed to the effects of measles infection. An outbreak of measles had hit Fort Leavenworth at about the time of the 4th of July celebration. Eleven Illinois volunteers had succumbed and several more troops later came down with the highly communicable disease. Even mild cases became more serious-

and occasionally fatal—as troops experienced unfamiliar living conditions and climate on the frontier. Captain Niles's remains were recovered and returned to Edwardsville. On October 15, 1847, the Alton Telegraph reported:

"Whereas the remains of our esteemed and lamented friend and fellow citizen, Captain Franklin Niles, who died on his route to Mexico on the 24th day of July last, while zealously engaged in vindicating the honor of our country, and upholding her arms in the war with Mexico, have been brought to this place, his adopted home,, where they are to remain forever…Throughout the entire proceedings, the deepest feelings seemed to pervade the community, well attesting the grief which the death of Captain Niles inspired amongst his numerous friends and acquaintances."[22]

Franklin Niles was remembered as "an excellent lawyer, remarkable for the facility with which he could prepare his papers and for the accuracy of his pleadings. Had Mr. Niles lived he would have become in all probability an eminent lawyer."[23.] Captain Niles left his widow Sarah Henrietta, and children Franklin, Elizabeth and Mary. Meanwhile, along the Santa Fe Trail, Colonel Newby had promoted J.H. Adams to the rank of captain and commander of Company I. Adams would be known as *"Captain Adams"* for the rest of his life and is still remembered as Captain Jack by descendants today.

The American southwest had been populated by native peoples for tens of thousands of years. From the fifteenth century, the area had been colonized as part of New Spain until Mexican independence. At the onset of war with Mexico, newly promoted Brigadier General Stephen W. Kearny, at the head of a force called Army of the West, marched from Fort Leavenworth to New Mexico, where he seized Santa Fe without a shot. He was followed by Colonel Sterling Price (later general) commanding the Second Missouri Mounted Volunteers and the only religious unit in American History, the Mormon Battalion. Kearny next marched overland, guided by Kit Carson, to California, where he was greatly responsible for securing California for the United States. Meanwhile Colonel Alexander Doniphan had marched east toward El Paso and Chihuahua. American forces were securing Mexican territory from Texas to the Pacific. The Illinois regiment was to reinforce and resupply U.S. troops remaining in the Santa Fe area.

The Santa Fe Trail, actually several southwest -leading routes, had become a heavily traveled military supply route by 1847. Forts were built to protect it. Troops were sent to these distant outposts to protect commercial traffic and civilian emigrants heading to New Mexico or California via the southern route. At the war's start, a train of one hundred wagons snaked down the trail to supply Bent's Fort in advance of the troops. Aside from environmental challenges and the hardships of the journey, the greatest threat along the trail came from hostile Native Americans. According to a report in the *St. Louis Reveille*, "The Indians attacked almost every train that crossed the plains in 1846 and 1847." [24.]

At Walnut Creek, a buffalo hunting party commanded by Captain Adams had a narrow escape. Buffalo meat was a welcome change from the daily ration of old bacon and beans. While resting on the sand hills along the Arkansas River, the party was surprised by a large number of Pawnee natives. The soldiers retreated to a small ridge and prepared to defend themselves. The soldiers held their fire as the Pawnee, now numbering perhaps two hundred paused. Captain Adams and the Pawnee chief confronted each other without weapons. With sign language they exchanged expressions of peace. However, while retreating from this meeting, the Indians wheeled and aggressively charged the soldiers. Adams ordered his men to form a skirmish line and hold their fire. About a couple hundred yards away, facing the ready muzzles of the soldiers' rifles, the Indians once again stopped short and turned back, allowing the troopers to return to their camp safely. Later that day, friendly Sac and Fox warriors said the war party of Pawnee Captain Adams had stared down intended to stampede the army cattle and kill any stray soldiers. The pickets and guard were doubled for the night.

Although harassed by natives periodically enroute with several narrow escapes, and one detachment of Missouri Volunteers being attacked and losing several head of livestock, there is no record of any trooper in Newby's Regiment being killed by hostile Indians.

If the Mexican War is seen as conflict between two nation states, we should also consider a third leg of the stool: non-state actors generically called Indians. After the 1830s, the workable peace agreements between Mexican settlers and the Comanche, Kiowa, Pawnee, Cheyenne, Arapaho, Apache and Navajo broke down. In the wake of extreme violence, many in the U.S. used Mexico's seeming inability to police Indian territory and safeguard their population as a reason to deny Mexican claims to its northern territories and enhance American expansion goals. Writing in his book, *War of a Thousand Deserts*, Brian DeLay recasts the narrative to shift emphasis to the Indians: "These fateful attitudes reached their logical conclusion in 1846 and 1847, when the United States invaded Mexico and exploited tensions and tragedies of the ongoing Indian war to more easily conquer the north and, critically, to discourage insurgency or guerilla war." [25]

By the end of July, Captain Adams had led his company to Council Grove, where the troops rested and a blacksmith was available to repair the wagons. The troops also drilled and took target practice, which was unusual and did not become standard procedure until after the Battle of the Little Big Horn in 1876. Muster rolls show Company I at Cedar Spring a month later on August 31. Colonel Newby reported his arrival in Santa Fe, along with six of his companies, on either the eleventh or thirteen of September.[26.] The march had consumed some ten weeks, including about two weeks of lay-by, covering an average of fifteen and a half miles a day.[27]

The Mexican town of Santa Fe sat at the head of a narrow valley on a branch of the Rio Grande River. The occupying American troops treated their stay in Santa Fe as *a fiesta,* with *fandango* dancing, music, local alcohol and, no doubt, Mexican *senoritas.* Colonel Newby issued strict disciplinary orders, and once Santa Fe was secured, he decided to split his forces to obtain more quarters for the men and forage for the animals. Acting as Department Commander and *de facto* military governor in the absence of General Price, away on leave, Colonel Newby launched a campaign against rear-guard Mexican troops gathering at Chihuahua. Captain Adams was ordered to San Phillipi (sic) (San Felipe), twenty-five miles north of Albuquerque enroute to El Paso. However,

Adams's Company neither reached Texas nor saw any enemy soldiers. Instead, I Company was recalled and rejoined the regiment at Santa Fe in January 1848. [28.] The Illinois soldiers, replaced by the Missouri Mounted Infantry in an obvious move of favoritism, marched back the four hundred miles unable to chase glory and full of indignation and disappointment.

Captain Adams clutched his blue woolen cape close to his neck in the night chill as he walked quickly between the wooden store fronts and thick adobe walled, flat roofed houses from the officer's mess to his own quarters. Looking down, he remembered to visit the civilian cobbler to have his worn boots repaired. His superior officers in the chain of command: Colonel Newby, Lieutenant Colonel Boyakin and Major Donalson regarded Adams well and had confidence in I Company. Adams had made friends among the other company commanders. A few officers from the Illinois and Missouri regiments had already been rotated home to serve as recruiting officers, as even more troops were being levied as replacements. Would his name be next? Troops under his command generally liked him and, more importantly, respected him. But garrison duties at winter quarters in Santa Fe bred disaffection among the troops. Even the marauding Indians ceased most hostilities in winter. Now acclimated to conditions in New Mexico, Captain Adams had come to even appreciate the stark desert landscape, the surrounding mountains with their chiseled marble canyons that had defied the Spanish conquistadors and sheltered the native tribes for centuries, the sudden storms that turned dry *arroyos* into raging torrents. He had learned a few phrases of Spanish, along with the coarser vocabulary of the American soldier. His interaction with the local population was primarily limited to the civilian contractors who supplied the military. He could even tolerate the chilies in all the food.

After months in the saddle, Captain Adams had become an able horseman, and he had occasionally sharpened his aim shooting at the human-figured saguaro cactus. News from home, perhaps next to food and ammunition a soldier's most important resource, was infrequent, but he was heartened to hear that his family was well in Edwardsville and wished him Godspeed home. News from the real battlefield arrived more regularly and seemed encouraging. Reports told of U.S. forces deep in the heart of Mexico winning victories and rolling up their mis-matched enemy on the push to Mexico City. Captain Adams's enlistment was until the end of the war. Would it all be over before I Company would be tested in battle?

In February, General Sterling returned to Santa Fe from leave and resumed command, with orders from Washington to take the offensive against Mexican troops threatening the west

Texas town of El. Paso. Sterling sent seven companies of infantry, supported by mounted dragoons and artillery to block the Mexican advance. U.S. troops next pushed the Mexican force out of Chihuahua and on March 16th, defeated the enemy at Santa Cruz de Rosales. It was the final battle of the Mexican War. I Company was not among those units deployed on the campaign.

However, with so many troops away at Chihuahua, it became impossible to guard the vast New Mexico territory from Indian raiders, now awakened from winter hibernation. Left in command at Santa Fe, Colonel Newby aggressively launched a spring campaign against the Navajo. For many of the Illinois volunteers, it would be their first and only military engagements—against arrows rather than Mexican cannon. After skirmishes in which several Navajos were killed while the U.S. troops suffered no casualties, the Indians sued a for peace and a treaty was negotiated.[29] Shortly thereafter, in June 1848, Lieutenant Colonel Boyakin and a detachment of Illinois volunteers (which included twenty-five men from Adams's Company) marched toward Zuni Pueblo to locate and free Navajo prisoners held there. Enroute, the troops encountered plentiful wild game: deer, antelope, wild turkeys and a young brown bear. They celebrated the Fourth of July with a barbeque feast near the summit of the Sierra Madre Mountains. Zuni

Pueblo, on the Colorado River about two hundred miles from Albuquerque (near present day Gallup, New Mexico) was home to an ancient pueblo people and the largest of New Mexico's pueblos. It had been "discovered" by Spaniards in 1539, searching for the fabled Seven Cities of Gold. It was home to about fifteen hundred Pueblo Indians. Approaching the town, Colonel Boyakin ordered his troops into line of battle, anticipating a fight. However, under a flag of truce, the Indians explained to the officers, including Captain Adams, that they held no Navajo prisoners and there was no need for a fight. (The Navajo and Zuni Pueblo people were fierce enemies and the Zunis had, in fact, killed any Navajo prisoners before the American arrival). Lieutenant Colonel Boyakin negotiated a treaty with Pueblo Governor Pedro Pico and Antonio Chapeton, "Commander of the War Parties of Zuni," guaranteeing protection of Zuni property and religious rights under the protection of civilian and military authorities in New Mexico and the United States for all time. Despite goodwill all around, the treaty was never forwarded to Washington for ratification.[30.] After returning to Albuquerque on around the first of August, the troops received news of the peace with Mexico. The Zuni Pueblo expedition was the last field action Newby's Regiment would see in the war.

Colonel Newby ordered his regiment to move out from Santa Fe on August 16. The troops filled their Mexican gourd canteens and packed their cotton haversacks, bid *adios* to their replacements, and retraced their steps along the Santa Fe Trail. Units began arriving back at Fort Leavenworth on September 18. Major Donalson arrived at the trail head by month's end with the last units to leave New Mexico. Only the steamboat trip back to Alton remained.

Captain Adams spent the river journey relaxing after the long march. However, after a year of Army service, he was not totally removed from danger. On October 6, the steamboat *Plowboy* carrying I Company hit a snag and began to sink. Even at autumn's lower ebb, the Missouri River remained a perilous channel full of runoff and all sorts of nature's debris. Fortunately, the accompanying steamer *Amelia* rescued all hands from the sinking boat and turbid water and proceeded to destination without further incident.[31]

The men of Newby's Regiment, Adams's Company were quickly discharged on October 16, 1848. In all, fifteen men from Adams's Company had died during the year, though none from enemy action. Five men had deserted, one at Alton before leaving and the other four at Ft. Leavenworth before the long march to the southwest. The rest dispersed with whatever stories of their service they had to tell and several months back-pay in their civilian pockets.

America's first foreign war had ended officially back on Feb. 2nd with the Treaty of Guadalupe Hidalgo. In one stroke Mexico surrendered more than half of its sovereign territory to the United States. By adding parts of present-day Arizona, California, Colorado, Nevada, New Mexico, Utah and Wyoming, the U.S. finally did stretch from sea to sea. The war had created presidents and military heroes. A generation of officers who would fight each other in the coming Civil War were forged in the Mexican crucible of war. For most, however, homecoming was a cheerful occasion but not one of welcoming conquering heroes. Folks in Illinois were as patriotic as anyone else, but the war had been controversial, fanning coals of antagonism over the issues of states' rights and slavery. Bleeding Kansas, John Brown, Dred Scott and the flash point election of President Abraham Lincoln from Illinois would all follow. But the returning veterans had more immediate concerns: families to reconnect with, lives to get on with, wounds both physical and mental to heal. By the turn of the twentieth century, the veterans of Adams's Company still had not received a government pension for their service. If the expansion of the country had been America's destiny, so be it.

Arriving home in Edwardsville, Captain J.H. Adams faced a destiny of his own.

Notes:

1. T.L. Hart, "To Arms! To Arms!," *SHEC Resources for Teachers*, https://shecashp.cuny.edu/items/show/1211, retrieved Nov. 28, 2021.

2. Isacc H. Elliot, *Record of the Services of Illinois Soldiers in the Black Hawk War 1831-32 and in the Mexican War 1846-48*, Springfield IL: Journal Company 1902.

3. "The Early History of Edwarsdsville," newspaper clippings, Beverly Bauser, Madison County IL GenWerb Coordinator.

4. Elliot, op. cit.

5. *History and Genealogy of the Pomeroy Family and Collateral Lines-England-Ireland-America comprising the Ancestors and Descendants of George Pomeroy of Pennsylvania*, William McL. And J. Nevin Pomeroy publishers, 1958.

6. Mary Z. Rose, Archival Research Manager, Madison County Historical Society, personal correspondence, Dec. 7, 2021.

7. "Old Landmarks Going," *Edwardsville Intelligenser*, Feb. 24, 1921.

8. *Edwardsville Madison County Courier*, Edwardsville Illinois, Feb. 15, 1866, p.3.

9. *Causes of Texas Independence*, https://www.exlors.com>summary>causes-of-Texas-Independence, retrieved Dec. 11, 2021.

10. Eugene C. Barker and James W. Pohil, "Texas Revolution," *Handbook of Texas*, Texas State

Historical Association,
https://www.tshaonline.org>handbook>entries>texas.

11. Phillip Thomas Tucker, *Exodus from the Alamo*, Philadelphia: Casemate Publishers, 2010, pp.9-61.

12. DrewVandeCreek, "TheMexicanAmericanWar," http://digital.lib.niu.edu/islandora/object/niu-lincoln%3A32025, retrieved Dec. 8, 2021.

13. Simon Winchester, *Land*, New York: Harper Perennial, 2022, p. 138.

14. John C. Pinheiro, "James K. Polk: Foreign Affairs," https://millercenter.org>president>foreignaffairs-affairs, retrieved Dec. 9, 2021.

15. "The Mexican War," Digital History, https://www.digitalhistory.uh.edu>disp-textbook, retrieved Dec. 7 2021.

16. Elliot, op.cit, pp. xxx-xxxi.

17. Lee Myers, "Illinois Volunteers in New Mexico, 1847-1848," New Mexico Historical Review 47, 1 (2021), https://digitalrepository.unm.edu/nmhr/vol47/iss1/2.

18. Alvin P. Stauffer, "The Quartermaster's Department and the Mexican War," *Quartermaster Review*, U.S. Army Quartermaster Foundation, May-June 1950, http://old.quartermasterfoundation.org>quartermaster, retrieved Dec. 10. 2021.

19. Ibid.

20. Meyers, op.cit.

21. David Cole, "Survey of U.S. Army Uniforms, Weapons and Accoutrements," from J. and S.G. Gideon, *General Regulations for the Army 1847*, Washington D.C. 1847,

https://history.army.mil>uniforms>survey, retrieved Nov. 30, 2021.

22. "Remains of Captain Franklin Niles Laid to Rest," *Alton Telegraph,* October 15, 1847, https://madison.illinoisgenweb.org>wars>MexicanAmerican, retrieved Nov 23, 2021.

23. *History of Madison County, Illinois*, W.R. Brink & Co., Edwardsville, Ill., 1882, p. 189.

24. *St. Louis Reveille,* June 3, 1848, in Walker D. Wyman, "The Military Phase of Santa Fe Freighting, 1846-1865," *Kansas Historical Journal,* Vol. 1, No. 5, November 1932, p. 420.

25. Brian DeLay, "It's Time to Remember the Role of Indians in the Mexican American War," History News Network, https://historynewsnetwork.org>article.

26. "Four Foot Soldiers on the Trail-An Illinois Odyssey,". https://wwwsantafetrailresearch.com>research>fourfoot soldiers on the trail, retrieved Dec. 16, 2021.

27. Myers, op.cit. p. 11.

28. Myers, Ibid. pp. 14-15.

29. Meyers. Ibid. pp. 20-21.

30. E. Richard Hart, *Pedro Pino: Governor of Zuni Pueblo 1830-1878*, University Press of Colorado 2003, in https://www.jstor.org>stable, pp. 21-22.

31. Myers, op. cit., p. 24.

Chapter 3

Argonauts

"Ho for California! The Overland Trek. California is really a land of gold and pearls."

–Fayette Robinson, Placerville, 1849

Captain Adams bore no war wounds and any psychological scars were minor. Like many veterans, he was usually reticent to talk about his military exploits. He preferred to focus on family and future. However, as proprietor of the general store he had ample occasion to swap stories with customers and even enchant young boys with anecdotes of soldiering and Indian fighting. Matilda noticed more about her husband than his toughened body wrapped in deeply weathered skin. He recognized authority and believed his own authority should be recognized by others. He possessed a firm ability to make command decisions and take disciplined action. And she would notice the far-away gaze in his eyes whenever he remembered the communion of his troops, the dust on the trail, the crack of the bullwhip, the confusion of gunfire. In a later era, after another war, the First World War song asked: *"How you gonna keep 'em down on the farm, after they've seen Paree?"* Santa Fe in the 1840s was certainly no Paris, but it stood for all the people, the places, the boundless opportunities waiting out there.

When news of the discovery of gold in California eventually found its way back to the populated part of the nation, it swept across the eastern states like a pandemic, infecting everyone with a gold fever. Captain John Hicks Adams was not immune. He already had a sense of California from stories of "The Pathfinder" John Fremont—possibly from the lips of famed scout Kit Carson, himself, while along the Santa Fe Trail, or from soldiers in the Missouri Battalion that had followed General Stephen Kearny to secure California in the early days of the war. And now that fabled land of milk and honey offered up gold for the taking. The siren song of *El Dorado,* the Golden One, wrenched people away from their homes and families in multitudes far beyond any military call-up of volunteers. Wagons west!

With time, California and the far west had become better known to Americans, if still exotic and distant. California had been colonized by Spain since the 16th century. The Spanish crown had supported the establishment of *presidios* (forts) and a string of Catholic missions to blunt Russian fur trading expansion from the northwest. But Spain found Alta (Upper) California almost too remote to administer. After Mexico achieved independence from Spain in 1821, its fragile new government secularized the original Franciscan missions in Alta (Upper) California and distributed the land to Mexican settlers or first-generation California -born *Californios* of Spanish descent. This created a society of some four or five hundred large *ranchos.* California's population was less than two thousand *Califorinio* adult males, mostly in the southern region of the territory, and a similar number of European and American immigrants clustered along the north-central coast and inland valleys. But many more Americans were on the move.

Missionaries had pushed west to Oregon by 1838. In 1839, a Swiss immigrant named Johann (John) Sutter managed to obtain ownership of a *rancho* in the Sacramento Valley of California, where he constructed a fort and built a fortune on raising crops and cattle. In 1841, the Bartleson-Bidwell party had traversed the Sonora Pass into California. Lansford Hastings had crossed the plains to Oregon in 1842 and then had come south into California before returning to Cincinnati, where he published *"Emigrants Guide to Oregon and California",* in which he extolled the virtues of California [1.] In 1844, the family of Irish immigrant Martin Murphy joined the wagon train of Elisha Stevens and headed west, following the wagon wheel ruts in the increasingly used Oregon Trail. The party found themselves blocked by the Sierra Nevada Mountains, until a native chief called Truckee showed them a pass over which they maneuvered their wagons with ropes. They survived the winter snows and arrived safely at Sutter's Fort near Sacramento, becoming the first Anglo settlers to successfully cross into California by land route. No one had died and a baby had been born along the way.

Another party of immigrants, the Donner -Reed Party, was not as fortunate as the Murphys, but their story became much more widely known and shocked the entire nation. Fearing winter snows due to their late departure from Illinois, the Donners choose to follow Lansford Hastings's short cut across the Utah desert. In fact, the route proved longer and by the time the party tried an alternate pass from the one used by the Murphys, they were caught in heavy snow. Facing starvation after four months trapped in the mountains, the Donners and Reeds resorted to cannibalism of their deceased in order to survive. Of the eighty-seven original members of the group, only forty-seven survived to be rescued in Spring 1847. The horrendous confluence of poor planning, bad decisions, bad timing and bad weather doomed the Donner-Reed Party to infamy and focused the reading public on the tribulations of crossing the Sierra in winter.[2]

Perhaps no one created more interest and influenced the direction of California history more than John Charles Fremont. A first-rate topographical engineer and military mind, Fremont made five expeditions into the west, beginning in 1842, most often guided by his life-long scout and friend Christopher "Kit" Carson. Fremont was also a masterful self-promoter and together with the inviting writing style of his wife Jessie Benton (daughter of "Manifest Destiny" champion Senator Thomas Hart Benton), he turned his scientific governmental reports of his journeys into a public relations coup that earned him the nickname "The Pathfinder."

In 1844, Fremont and Carson led an expedition south from Oregon and slipped into Mexican California over the Sierra, by way of a pass that bears Kit Carson's name. They viewed from a distance the pristine Alpine Lake later known as Tahoe, possibly the first non-native Americans to see it. While resting at Sutter's Fort, Fremont sensed the weakness of Mexican authority. Subsequently, he made another clandestine journey to California the following year to advance American interests. After withdrawing his small force to Oregon, he returned and supported the so-called Bear Flag Revolt by a group of American insurgents against Mexican authority, creating the California Republic. Styling himself Military Commander of U.S. Forces in California, he stayed on to play a leading role in the politics and fighting that ensued with the Mexican War. After a contentious court martial in 1848, Fremont retired to his enormous *Rancho Las Mariposas* near Yosemite, where a major gold strike created instant riches for himself. His career continued as U.S. senator from California, unsuccessful Republican candidate for the presidency in 1856, Commanding General of the Department of the West during the Civil War, and governor of the Arizona Territory. Though controversial, countless counties, cities, topographical features, schools, streets and organizations are named for this larger-than-life persona.

By 1848, America seemed to have gained its equilibrium. Mormon followers of Brigham Young had crossed into the Valley of the Great Salt Lake and established their colony a year earlier. The Mexican War concluded with the enormous land acquisition under the Treaty of Guadalupe Hidalgo, and the conflict with Britain over Oregon had been settled diplomatically. But then, on January 24,1848, the genie escaped from the lamp, and everything changed. While supervising construction of a sawmill for John Sutter on the American River in the foothills of the Sierra, James Marshall spotted that bright shiny object in the muddy gravel of the riverbank: flecks of gold nugget. It was a secret impossible to keep. Rumors of the discovery began to spread throughout California. The safe harbor town of Yerba Buena, becoming known as San Francisco, began emptying of men as they rushed for the gold fields, only to be replaced by legions of more gold seekers over the next couple of years. Soon ships sailing between Pacific ports from Mexico to Oregon leaked word of the find. In those days when communication was tightly tied to transportation, even Hawaiians heard the news before the eastern United States.

By early summer, rumors of the gold strike started to percolate through to the rest of America. At first, with no reporters on the ground in California, the eastern press remained skeptical, But the news trickle became a flood. *The New York Herald, New York Daily Tribune* and *The Evening Post* began reprinting letters from California, detailing great fortunes to be made, but also describing the downside hardships and disappointments. By fall, the press reported the discovery of gold as fact and the rush was on.[3.] Within the year, tens of thousands of would -be miners and fortune seekers from all points of the globe were headed to the California gold fields.

Local and regional newspapers, then as now, picked up the New York reporting. Illinois citizens followed news from

California closely. The ill-fated Donner-Reed Party had originated in Springfield. News from California spurred a Springfield group to form The Illinois and California Mutual Insurance Company, to supply the gold miners and leave in March,1849. Apparently, California and the west even piqued the interest of Abraham Lincoln. Among those who left Illinois for the Pacific coast was his tailor, Benjamin Biddle. William Ide, who led the Bear Flag Revolt in 1846 and became first governor of the California Republic was also a Lincoln associate. And William L. Todd of Edwardsville, Mary Todd Lincoln's cousin, designed the California Bear Flag, still flying over the state capitol in Sacramento.[4] In 1849, Lincoln was offered the governorship of Oregon, an idea quickly quashed by Mrs. Lincoln.[5] (A different decision would have denied America its greatest president. But California was never far from Lincoln's mind. Toward the close of the Civil War, he acknowledged the contribution of California gold to the war effort. Enroute to Ford's theater on April 14, 1865, he is said to have mused aloud of fulfilling his dream of seeing California after his presidency, a dream and a nation all shattered by John Wilkes Booth.)

Many 49ers, as they became called, made the journey to the gold fields by packet steamer to Central America, then crossed the narrow Isthmus of Panama by mule or canoe, continuing up the Pacific coast by steamer again. Others opted for the less expensive, but longer and slower, voyage around the tip of South America and on to San Francisco. However, Midwesterners more often chose the overland route that became known as the California Trail. The lessons instilled by the tragedy of the Donner Party's late start were well learned. With the advent of spring, nourishing prairie grass for the animals and freshwater runoff would be most plentiful and put the argonauts (named for the mythological quest by Jason for the golden fleece) into the Sierra before the winter snows (although it also placed them in the Great Basin Desert in midsummer). Scores of heartland emigrants were already passing through Alton and Edwardsville on their way to gateway gathering points in St. Louis, Independence and St. Joseph.

Home from the war barely six months, Captain J.H. Adams once again prepared to leave-and prepared his family for his absence. Matilda was again pregnant. (Sarah Jane Adams, born while her father headed west, would one day marry Donner Party survivor James "jimmy" Frazier Reed Jr.). On April 4, 1849, Captain Adams executed a deed of conveyance to Henry K. Eaton in return for $290, divesting some of his inherited property from his fatrher.[6.] In June, the *Alton Telegraph* published a notice by Captain Hicks and

63

attorneys J. and D. Gillespie, announcing his intention as administrator of his father's estate, to apply for a circuit court order at their August term to sell any or all of his interest in the estate to satisfy any debts outstanding, and he invited his siblings to also appear and do likewise.[7] By the summer court session, Captain Hicks would already be headed to California, leaving the Gillespies with power of attorney, but obviously he was putting his own affairs in order. Whatever promises, protestations or shared dreams of striking it rich transpired in the Adams's' household, Captain Adams was among the first in his community to follow his own dreams once again.

On the 8th of April 1849, Captain Adams hitched a team of six mules to his wagon. He favored mules over oxen because they traveled faster and were more durable on rough terrain. Horses were too expensive, and mules could prove useful at the destination. Their "prairie schooners" wagon was smaller than the Conestoga wagons used in the east to carry freight. He had fit bows of hickory over his open wagon and stretched heavy cotton, waterproofed with linseed oil, over the bows to form a cover. The wagon wheels, six feet in diameter in the rear and four in the front for sharper turning, were newly rimmed with iron. As a former regimental quartermaster, Captain Adams instinctively knew how best to load the wagon, keeping its center of gravity low to avoid tipping over. He double checked the inventory: foodstuffs, toolbox, ammunition, canvas tents, spare wood, metal and leather parts for repairs, a barrel for water, a can of tar mixed with animal fat to keep the axels greased. He knew the lighter the load, the easier and safer the journey. They would pass countless discarded items along the trail.

Three other men accompanied Captain Adams: his brother-in-law Allen Pomeroy; William Bolden Reynolds, a former Madison County Commissioner; and Dr. Charles Marion Lusk. Dr. Lusk had graduated in medicine in Louisville, Kentucky and practiced next door to his father's hotel in Edwardsville. (After arriving in California, Dr. Lusk would be recruited by a Mexican planter to fight epidemic fever in Mexico at the princely sum of $100 per day. After returning to practice medicine in San Francisco for a few years, he returned to Illinois via Panama and was a highly regarded physician in Edwardsville until his death in 1863.[8)] Because the wagon could only accommodate one person in the box, the Adams Party likely walked alongside the wagon and mules, although they may have shared a horse. Many horses succumbed to the journey and died along the California Trail and were the primary target of Indian raids.

The first leg of the journey was uneventful. They shipped their wagon and provisions by steamer from St. Louis to St.

Joseph, on the Missouri River, while driving their team of animals by land straight across Missouri to St. Joseph, the staging point for wagons heading west. Because selecting the best jumping-off point was the first major decision emigrants had to make, and could set the tone for the entire journey, cities such as Independence, Weston, Westport and St. Joseph competed to attract the business of the nearly half million emigrants headed for the west. Some arrived at these portals by boat, others by land. Some were fully equipped, others not at all. The *St. Joseph Gazette* of March 2, 1849 claimed: "Goods could be purchased as reasonably in St. Joseph as in Lexington or Independence; that St. Joseph was many miles nearer to the destination; that its route was not only shorter but superior because there were no major rivers or streams to cross"[9] Built on the site of a former fur trading post, St. Joseph had remained small until the spread of gold fever. By 1849 it offered dozens of dry-goods stores, blacksmiths, livery stables, saloons, restaurants, brothels and purveyors of all kinds to meet the emigrants' supply needs. Hotels were overflowing and most emigrants camped away from the bustling commercial center. "Thousands of settlers arrived by steamboat, while hundreds of wagon trains lined the streets waiting to be ferried across the Missouri River. In 1849 alone, some have estimated that as many as 50,000 pioneers passed through St. Joseph. The city quickly became a bustling outpost and rough frontier town, as covered wagons, oxen and supplies purchased by the emigrants established the economic basis for the city." [10]

After outfitting themselves one last time, the Edwardsville quartet joined a company of other emigrants from Edwardsville, organized military-style with captains. Whether Captain Adams was recruited to help marshal the civilian army or not is not known. These groupings were necessary for safety, herding the animals and mutual aid during breakdowns. Wagon trains could number in the dozens or more and stretch for miles across the prairie. Larger trains were prone to more discord and journeys that lasted up to six months while smaller wagon clusters tended to be more homogeneous and harmonious, reaching their destination sooner. Given the Adams party arrival in California after less than four months, they likely traveled small and traveled light.

Crossing into Kansas, bugle calls must have sounded in Captain Adams's memory, but the only sounds now were the creaking of covered wagons and the snorting of livestock as they picked up the Little Blue River into Nebraska. The local Indians here were Pawnee, not Navajo. The Oregon-California Trail wasn't a single well-defined thoroughfare. Rather it was a wide swath of mostly parallel tracks that became more distinct with each rumbling wagon, usually converging at bottleneck river crossings or narrow mountain passes. Instead of road signs and trail markers, the pathway was littered with discarded goods and abandoned broken-down wagons, the farther west the greater the debris field and number of carcasses of dead animals.

Emigrants cooked their food over sage brush or buffalo chips fires or ate it cold. While a child might find room inside a wagon to sleep, most everyone slept under the wagons or rough under a canopy of prairie stars. Few emigrants were prepared for the extreme swings in temperature in a single day. Torrential thunderstorms, accompanied by apocalyptic lightning turned the trail into a grand boulevard of sucking mud and made trickling creeks suddenly impassable. Even when nature accommodated, Indian raiders were a constant threat and occasional reality. A diary entry by F.F. Keith recorded, "Mon morning the Indians stole more horses from a train just below us and killed one man and scalped him their chief came riding near the camp when they fired upon him putting three balls through him before he fell about 40 men then pursued them to the mountains but could do nothing with them as the horses of the Indians are fresh while the emigrants are nearly worn out. [sic}"[11]

Whether the emigrants were headed to Oregon, the Valley of the Great Salt Lake or, after 1848, the California gold fields, everyone took the same route. They followed the valleys of the Platte and North Platte Rivers westward across the Great Plains, circumvented the Rocky Mountains, and followed the Sweetwater River to South Pass. The first thousand miles were relatively flat, and this first leg of the journey was the easier half. [12]

Many travelers along the trail kept journals or wrote letters that would later be published in hometown newspapers, detailing their trip in vivid detail. Unfortunately, Adams and company did not commit their experiences for the public record. But from words of fellow travelers, and because so many made the same journey, a vivid accounting of life on the trail exists today. One major threat was cholera, which followed the wagon trains from Missouri westward like a hovering shroud. "in the height of the migration, from 4,000 to 5,000 emigrants died of this pestilence; and if there was a half mile which the Indians had failed to punctuate with a grave, the cholera took care to remedy the omission." [13]

"If an emigrant escaped the cholera, crossed all the rivers in safety, if he was beyond the muddy region and a fortunate shower had laid the dust for a time, still the voracious mosquitoes hovered about to prey upon him." [14] " Of much greater concern was the dearth of grass and good water. Much of the water along the route was highly impregnated with alkali and almost unfit for use. The comparatively small bodies of emigrants who crossed the plains and mountains prior to 1849 fared much better in securing grass than those of later years. When oxen and cattle began to follow the trail by the tens of thousands the problem of sustenance became a vital one. The three most frequently mentioned articles in an emigrant's journal or diary are water, grass and fuel. When nothing better was available, the emigrants had to drink out of mud puddles, buffalo wallows or whatever happened to be at hand."[15]

After leaving Fort Kearny on the Platte River, the Adams Party would have measured their progress by geological formations such as Chimney Rock, Nebraska, a cone and spire visible for miles above the plain. Typical mule trains covered between ten and fifteen miles a day, punctuated by days of rest. Wagon trains played leapfrog with each other as they walked or rested. After passing Scotts Bluff, Nebraska, they passed into Wyoming. After pausing at Fort Laramie, the train pushed on into the Crow Indian Territory and the Black Hills. It's likely they encountered Independence Rock by sometime in June, but no later than Independence Day. This granite monolith was so named as a destination to be reached by the Fourth of July in order to safely reach California before snowfall, and the Adams Party would cross the Sierra by mid-summer, safely ahead of schedule. Leaving the red granite buttes and sage covered plains of the Black Hills, the Sweet Water River led them to the South Pass through the Rockies.[16]

At South Pass, emigrants reached the half-way mark, crossing the Continental Divide. "South Pass, 7,550 feet above sea level, was the great tipping point on the westward journey. Here, the division of waters, Atlantic versus Pacific, signified the cleaving of one's life. The past lay east, the future west-and for many emigrants, there would be no returning. "[17.] At this juncture, the trail split off northwest to Oregon and generally southwest along several routes to California, all leading to the Humboldt River. It would be the hardest five hundred miles of the journey.

After leaving South Pass California-bound emigrants bid adieu to those continuing to Oregon. Bypassing the Salt Lake Cutoff and following the Sublette Cutoff to Soda Springs, Granite Pass and Humboldt Wells, they eventually reached the Humboldt River in modern Nevada, before encountering forty miles of arid desert moonscape and the Carson and Humboldt Sinks. More suffering and animal death occurred in these forty miles than on any other part of the journey, mostly in the sand dunes that block the final miles to either (Truckee or Carson) river. [17.] Here, where trickling rivers literally came to die, disappearing into sandy desert oblivion, the trail was clearly marked with scores of desiccated and putrefying animal

71

carcasses, as well as the last remnants of discarded belongings and vehicles from previous emigrants. Emigrant David Wooster wrote: "We took a supply of water for about ten miles only, and thirty of us started across what we found to be a second desert. We found it twenty-eight miles. Our horses lay down several times; some of the men could get no farther, but waited six miles back, till water could be brought...my canteen was empty the first seven miles, and never did human being suffer more than myself; but I got through without stopping, halfdead."[18]

Beyond the last watering place before the desert between the Humboldt Sink and the Carson River, the temperatures soared, and the animals nearly gave out after eating nothing but sparse alkali grass with little water. They were unable to pull the wagon through the heavy sand. Captain Adams decided to unhitch the team and drive them loose from the wagon to the Carson River and water, then return for the wagon, with Adams, himself, staying behind. As the others from Adams's party headed for the Carson River, Indians killed one of the mules and others suffered arrow wounds. Meanwhile Captain Adams dug a hole deep enough to find brackish water at the sandy bottom. He made coffee to hide the taste of the water. He remained camped alone by their wagon for two nights before his companions returned. With rejuvenated animals, they pulled the wagon across the last of the desert.[19]

Parched and exhausted, the emigrants reached the Carson River, named for the legendary scout, Taking the trail southwesterly through the Carson Valley, the Party would have entered the formidable, but incredibly beautiful landscape of the Carson River canyon, which opened like a hallway into the foothills of the eastern Sierra Nevada and coming to the foyer, now called Hope Valley. In midsummer the group found plentiful forage, and water. They rested several days, allowing the animals to revive and regain strength. Only one final challenge lie ahead, the ascent of the majestic Sierra.

Once an ancient seabed, North America moved away from the mega-continent of Pangaea some two hundred-plus million years ago. As the North American plate overrode the ocean floor plate, it added "vast amounts of new land to North America's western edge" and threw up the towering volcanic Sierra Nevada Mountain range that stops any Pacific moisture from crossing east into the Great Basin of modern Utah and Nevada. [20]

In 1844, Indians had told Fremont and Carson of a way though the Sierra but also warned them of winter snow. The Donner Party had chosen the alternate Truckee River route and disaster followed. In 1848, members of the Mormon Battalion

73

who had served a year's military service in California during the Mexican War, had regrouped at Sutter's Fort. Several had been working with James Marshall at Sutter's Mill. In order to return to Salt Lake City, these Mormons had hewn a trail between the west fork of the Carson River and the south fork of the American River, where Fremont and Carson had first explored. This Carson pass avoided most all the Truckee River crossings and switchbacks and dropped directly down to the gold fields at Hangtown. As the Adams party jostled through the pine forests and mountain meadows ablaze in purple lupin and yellow mules' ears on the final arduous descent into California, they were among the estimated twenty-five to fifty thousand gold seekers who had made the epic trip just in 1849-many more thousands would follow-and, as the saying of the day went: *they had seen the elephant.*

Notes:

1. *Lincoln's Springfield: Letters from California and Oregon (1845-52),* Spring Creek Series, Richard E. Hart, ed., Springfield, Illinois, 2020, p. 14.

2. "Donner and Reed Wagon Train Incident," National Park Service, https://www.nps.gov>cali>learn>historyculture, retrieved Dec. 1, 2021.

3. Barry L. Dutka, "New York Discovers Gold! In California," *California History,* University of California Press, Vol. 63, No. 4 (Fall 1984), p. 319.

4. *Lincoln's Springfield: Letters from California and Oregon (1845-52),* op. cit.

5. Rowland R. Gittings, "Abraham Lincoln Once Declined Governorship of Oregon," *The Oregon Sunday Journal,* February 11, 1912, http://www.ochcom.org>pdf>Lincoln-OR-Gov, retrieved December 30, 2021.

6. John Hicks Adams, Deed of Conveyance, April 4, 1849, Madison County Historical Society.

7. *Alton Telegraph,* Alton, Illinois, June 22, 1849, p. 4.

8. Jessie Evelyn Springer, *Charles Springer of Cranehook-on-the Delaware: His descendants and allied families,* Edwardsville: September 28, 1959.

9. *St. Joseph Gazette,* March 2, 1849, in Crossing at St. Joseph, Oregon-California Trails Association, https://www.gateway-octa.org>trail-history, retrieved November 30, 2021,

10. "St. Joseph, Missouri – Jumping Off To The West," *Legends of the West,*

https://www.legendsofamerica.com>mo-stjoseph, retrieved November 30, 2021.

11. Fluery F. Keith, "Diary, Monday, August 18, 1850," p. 11 in Michael N. Landon, "Chasing a Golden Dream: The Story of the California Trail," http://overlandtrails.lib.byu.edu>essay-ctrail, retrieved Dec. 1, 2021.

12. Keith Heyer Meldahl, *Hard Road West, History and Geology along the Gold Rush Trail*, (Chicago) University of Chicago Press, 2007. P. 229.

13. Charles F. Lummis, "Pioneer Transportation in America," *McClure's Magazine,* Vol. XXVI, p. 83, in Amos William Hartman, " The California and Oregon Trail," 1849-1860, *The Quarterly of the Oregon Historical Society,* Vol. XXV, No. 1, March 1924, on http://www:jstor.org/stable/20610264, retrieved Nov. 30, 2021.

14. Hartman, op cit., p. 13.

15. Ibid. p. 13-14.

16. Stewart Johnston, Map of Oregon Trail and Route to the California Gold Rush along the Humboldt River, map 1893, in https://texashistory.unt.edu/ark/67531/metaph193547/m1/1/:>Arlington Library, retrieved Nov. 30, 2021.

17. Keith Heyer Meldahl, op. cit. p.105.

18. David Wooster, Letter, *The Gold Rush: letters of David Wooster from California to the* Adrian, Michigan, Expositor *1850-1855*, ed. John Cumming, Mount Pleasant, MI: The Cumming Press, 1972, in Michael N. Landon, op cit.

19. "Capt. John H. Adams, a Mexican Veteran and a 49-er – An Adventurous Life," *San Jose Pioneer Press*, 1878.

20. Keith Heyer Meldahl, op. cit. p. 120.

Chapter 4
Old Dry Diggins

"Thou shalt not tell any false tales about good diggings in the mountains."

–James Hutchings,
The Miner's Ten Commandments,
Placerville, 1853

The gold that eroded out of California bedrock and sank to the bottom of streams or clung in veins of quartz triggered a tsunami of population migration worldwide. The first to rush to the Sierra Nevada foothills were local Anglo settlers and *Californios* (Mexicans born in California) as well as a few Mai-du or Miwok natives. The Miwoks were a gentle people ill served by the newcomers pouring into California. As the news spread, others followed from the Americas, the Pacific and eventually Europe and Asia. By the summer of 1848, more than a thousand miners had already descended on the Coloma discovery site; an estimated eighty-thousand immigrants streamed into California during the first year after discovery. "In the ten years that followed the rush of '49,

79

miners sifted, scraped and blasted 28 million ounces of gold out of the Sierra Nevada foothills. It was by far the greatest concentrated gold strike in human history up to that point, worth $594 million at the time (more than $10 billion today) .... the biggest strikes were made by a comparative few. Many more wandered from one barren digging to another, sometimes for years, growing ever more impoverished and disillusioned." [1]

Crude mining camps quickly spread north and south from Coloma like charms on a bracelet. Tents and hastily erected shelters built from any materials available sprung like spring mushrooms in isolated mining clusters with names like Gold Hill, Murderer's Bar, Shingle Springs and Old Dry Diggins. Old Dry Diggins got its colorful name because miners had to cart dry dirt and rock down to the nearby creek to wash out any gold. Old Dry Diggins was located at a crossroads of the north-south run of the gold bearing Mother Lode, and on the east-west track down from Carson Pass to Sacramento. The evening of August 1, 1849, after he arrived at Old Dry Diggins, Captain John Hicks Adams panned out about fifty cents worth of gold dust from the creek bank and mailed it home to Matilda with news of his arrival.

Old Dry Diggins soon received an even more colorful name: Hangtown. Even in the earliest days after the strike when gold was plentiful to find, competition between miners was fierce. Often, disputes were settled with violence. Assault, robbery and murder were commonplace. "The miners quickly became short tempered with the rising crime rate and the lack of readily-available law enforcement, so they took the "law" (or lack thereof) into their own hands. Criminals were punished in short order whether it be by flogging or hanging, based on snap decisions made by impromptu courts with hastily formed juries." [2]

The first hangings meted out by vigilante justice in the mining camps had occurred in early 1849. A trio of poker players in a make-shift saloon robbed the proprietor of his gold dust at gunpoint. After apprehending the robbers, a miners' court sentenced them to be flogged. According to the *Sacramento Daily Union*, "The criminals were then ordered to leave. In a few days, two of the men, under the influence of whisky, went about the camp intimating that the men who were engaged in the trial were "spotted", that "they would not live to flog another man," etc. A meeting was called, the two men were arrested and hung on the leaning oak tree in the yard below Elstner's El Dorado Saloon, the same tree on which, afterwards, other malefactors expiated their crimes. For many years the town went by the name Hangtown to distinguish it from other dry diggings."[3.] Hangtown continued to grow as an important transportation hub, being renamed once again to the less macabre Placerville in 1854. The town grew to become California's third largest city behind San Francisco and Sacramento (Los Angeles remained merely a small, dusty *pueblo)*. It became an important stop for the short-lived Pony Express and as a stop for stagecoaches hauling passengers, freight and later silver from the Comstock Lode in Nevada, which would involve John Hicks Adams directly in the decade ahead. Nevertheless, the "Hangtown" nickname has endured. In 2021, the Placerville City Council unanimously voted to retain the "Hangtown" nickname, although bowing to twenty-first century political sensibilities, the council voted to remove the hangman's noose from the city's logo.

Captain Adams and party left Hangtown on the second day for Cold Springs on Weber Creek, and then on to Coloma, near the discovery site. He then headed to Sacramento where he sold his team and wagon and bought food and mining supplies. Accompanying the freight wagon back to the gold fields, Captain Adams detoured to observe miners at Mormon Island in the American River using rockers to wash out the gold. At sundown, he was intercepted by three Mexicans, also on foot, who threatened him with a short sword and demanded his money, about $800 in dust and coin from the sale of his wagon and team. Captain Adams, having left his large Allen revolver in the freight wagon, feigned a weapon inside his pocket and kept walking, telling the robbers his companions were nearby and that they had better leave the area. Pretending to listen for his wagon, Captain Adams bluffed the Mexicans into inaction and safely defused the confrontation. Arriving back at Coloma, money intact and the provisions having arrived, he joined his friends mining a bar near the old Sutter mill, pulling about $20 apiece out of the river each day for the next few weeks.[4]

Captain Adams, along with Allen Pomeroy continued to mine near Coloma. Other members of his party scattered to other locations. Dr. C. M. Lusk relocated in Sacramento, again practicing medicine. Ed. Milner, who had traveled west with the Adams party, filed claims at Canyon Creek, about fourteen miles form Coloma, near present Georgetown, and encouraged Adams to join him there. Having found a promising seam of gold at Coloma, Adams and Pomeroy stayed. Meanwhile Milner and his partners found enough gold to return to Georgia that first fall with about $40,000 each, while the Coloma strike yielded less than a tenth of that before petering out.[5]

In the fall of 1849, after the first heavy rains turned the flats into a quagmire and the creeks rose too high to work, the party moved up the ridge to an area near present Georgetown and built a cabin. By November they were joined by other men from Illinois, including Major G.W. Hook, who had also been a company commander of the Fifth Illinois Volunteers during the Mexican War. Given the exorbitant prices for provisions and supplies in the mining camps, especially in winter, Captain Adams seized an opportunity, purchased several extra mules and began running pack trains through the Mother Lode. "Every conceivable item needed to be brought in and pack trains were indispensable...Mexican mules were stronger, tougher and possessed more endurance. The average train consisted of 40 to 50 mules with two muleteers...within a few years the network of trails developed into roads."[6]

On one run, Adams fell ill and stayed behind, letting young assistant Edward Bualt drive the mules, along with Allen Pomeroy and a man named Whittenberg. That night the first snow fell while the party slept. Indians surrounded the campsite, stole the mules and rained arrows on the sleeping men, wounding all three. Mr. Whittenberg's wounds were the least serious. Pomeroy was severely wounded in the leg. Bault was pierced deeply under his arm by an arrow and fainted after Pomeroy pulled it out. A passing pack train took word of the attack to Captain Adams's cabin and Adams set out to rescue them, accompanied by Major Hook and two other men. They found their injured friends alive but too weakened to walk and the snow deepening by the minute. When the mules could no longer negotiate the snow, the wounded Bault was transported by shoulder litter. At the end of the third day, the party staggered out of the drifts and into their Georgetown cabin, where other miners waited with a roaring fire and food for the rescue party. A waiting doctor pronounced Bault's wounds mortal, and he died after a week of suffering. He was the first American buried on the Georgetown Divide.

In fact, Indians were not the greatest danger to be faced in the forested foothills of the gold country. Grizzly bears abounded, so plentiful that the ursine image had been incorporated into the rebels' flag during the 1846 Bear Flag Revolt and remains the central design of the California state flag. Once while tracking deer, Captain Adams encountered three men running hard from a wounded bear in pursuit. Following bloody tracks in the snow, Captain Adams came face to face with the giant grizzly, squatting over another man. Adams raised his rifle, but it misfired. The bear turned toward the captain, growling in anger and pain. With no chance to reload, Adams stood his ground until another man ran up, startling the animal which then ran off into the scrub brush and trees, freeing his captive unhurt but badly shaken. Whether staring down Pawnee warriors, bandits or bears, Captain Adams demonstrated nerves of steel.

Miners first began working the Georgetown District in 1849. Many quartz veins, with concentrations of gold in the seams, were worked by placer mining (washing our particles of gold from deposits of gravel or sand). One seam at the Georgia Slide mining site was said to measure 1,000 feet long by 500 feet wide. The town of Georgetown was originally known as Growlersburg, possibly because of large nuggets growling in the miners' pans—or maybe it was the miners growling. There are a couple candidates named George who may have given the town its later name.

The Indian raid had cost Captain Adams several of his expensive mules and ended his mule train packing business. He stayed the winter of 1849 at Canyon Creek but by spring he wandered about the north and middle forks of the American River, looking for a favorable, undisturbed site to mine. On May 1, 1850, he joined a party of prospectors to explore Lake Tahoe. Originally "discovered"-and then ignored - by the 1844 Fremont expedition, which misjudged its 21-mile length and western outlet, the large fresh-water lake had long been an important part of Washoe Indian life, its name, *Tahoe,* a corruption of the Washoe word *Da ow a ga,* or "edge of the lake".

Few Euro-Americans ventured into Tahoe. Emigrants crossing the region stayed on the most popular and well-established trails and had no defined route to draw them through the Tahoe Basin. A gold seeker visited briefly in 1850 and was followed months later by another gold-seeking party [including Adams]. Neither found their illusionary *El Dorado* but reported back about the extraordinarily scenic high-altitude lake. [7.] In 1872, author Mark Twain in his book *Roughing It* would recall his first glimpse of Lake Tahoe in 1861: "I thought it must surely be the fairest picture the whole world affords."[8]

Although his diggings near Georgetown were panning out, Captain Adams moved south from El Dorado County to Dry Creek in Calaveras County, made famous by Mark Twain's *The Jumping Frog of Caleveras County. Calaveras* is the Spanish word for skulls, due to the number of human remains found along the lower reaches of the river. The mining camp at Dry Creek was called Dry Town, after the creek running dry in summer - but not the town, which featured more than two dozen saloons by the early 1850s. With a population of a few hundred miners in tents and cabins along the creek, the village offered taverns, stores, butcher shops and gambling, as well as access to generous diggings.[9.] In Dry Town, he fell back on his Illinois mercantile roots and, in partnership with Louis Bualt (cousin to the deceased Ed. Bualt) opened a store and hotel. Anticipating another winter of heavy snows and rain, they laid in a large inventory priced to sell at high margin. Unfortunately, a mild winter ensued, dampening demand and cutting sharply into any profit. By spring, Captain Adams had cut his losses, divested his interests in the business and nearby mining claim (he retained interest in the Georgetown strike, operated by Allen Pomeroy) and moved down to Sacramento.[10.] He once again found hauling freight and supplies up to the mining camps lucrative.

Only a minority of 49ers actually struck it rich. Gold mining was extremely hard work and often dangerous. Lack of adequate housing, sanitation and health care challenged even the strongest constitutions. Law enforcement and public safety hardly existed. Such necessities as food proved incredibly expensive. While fortunes could be found on any given morning, they could just as easily be lost that evening at cards or at the point of a Bowie knife. The hope of a lucky strike drove many prospectors on, but many more gave up in despair and returned home busted or remained in California, starting over. Many of the fortunes made during the gold rush were accumulated by entrepreneurs fulfilling miners' needs rather than doing the back-breaking digging themselves. Mormon leader Sam Brannan, who was one of the first to hear rumors of Marshall's discovery while at Sutter's Fort, and then announced it widely in San Francisco, quickly bought up all available picks, shovels and pans and sold them to the hordes rushing to the gold fields, thereby becoming California's first millionaire. An Immigrant named Levi Strauss ran a dry goods business in San Francisco and later manufactured durable pants out of Genoa cloth ("jeans"), reinforced with metal rivets, and built an iconic business still in operation A Placerville purveyor of groceries and hardware named Leland Stanford compounded his profits, eventually becoming one of the Big Four tycoons of the transcontinental railroad, governor and senator from California, and philanthropist endowing a university in memory of his son. Scores more recognized that the gold deposits would become depleted or increasingly difficult to extract and turned their attention to the west's most valuable asset: vast tracts of highly fertile agricultural land.

For others, however, the legacy of the gold rush was a disaster. Greed often brought out the worst in people. Competition for claims pitted miners against one another, and Anglos in general against indigenous people, Mexicans, Chinese *celestials* seeking the "Gold Mountain" and all other foreigners - first with prejudicial tax policies, exclusionary immigration laws and then more violent expressions of ethnic prejudice. California's first governor, Peter H. Burnett, called for the removal or extinction of native Americans and offered bounties for scalps. The environment suffered no less. Vast hillsides were reduced to muddy rubble. Water supplies were poisoned, and forests clear-cut for lumber.[11]

Simon Winchester characterized the 49er prospectors as *"wholly disdainful of the Indians...They saw it as their right as the new Californians to enter Miwok lands with impunity, there to plunder this or that lode....As it happened, the places where most gold was to be found were on the very same acres where wild game was the most abundant – just below the Sierra winter snow line – and so were the most thickly populated with Miwok villages. It is scarcely surprising that from time to time the Native Americans raised objection to the strangers' ruin of their traditional lands, and that from time to time they fought back."*[12]

Captain Adams was among those who saw their future in California and had enough gold dust in their pockets to make it happen. He sold out his freighting concern in September 1851 and headed for San Francisco. The previously peaceful settlement, shrouded in grey fog between the bay and the ocean, had exploded into a booming tangle of wooden houses, hotels and restaurants and bustling commercial buildings. Not yet the bawdy Barbary Coast it would become, San Francisco nevertheless offered diversion and enterprise to anyone who had the nuggets to pay, and dreams for those who didn't. But he didn't linger. Almost immediately, he exercised the more costly, but quicker, travel option and purchased ship's passage to Panama, and hence across the isthmus, to New Orleans, up the Mississippi and on to Edwardsville. He was going home to his family in Illinois, but he would bring them back to California.

Although the greatest number of emigrants from the eastern United States traveled overland to California, and heavy freight was shipped around Cape Horn at the tip of South America, "for over twenty years, the lifeline which bound the Pacific Coast of the United States with the rest of the nation lay over the Isthmus of Panama. The route from New York and New Orleans to San Francisco and Oregon by way of the Isthmus was that over which mail, news, express, treasure and passengers were transported from 1848 until the completion of the Central Pacific-Union Pacific Railroad in 1869." [13] For would be gold-seekers, speed was essential. In 1848, Congress authorized establishment of two steamship lines to transport mail between New York and San Francisco: The U.S. Mail Steam Line on the Atlantic, with ports in Charleston, Savannah, New Orleans, Havana and Chagres, and on the Pacific coast the Pacific Mail Steamship Company sailing between Panama City and Monterey, San Francisco and Astoria, Oregon. During the gold rush, these shipping companies played a key role in moving goods, mail and passengers, and in developing San Francisco into a major city.

"Here is one of the great ironies of history: Departing from New York before the discovery of gold in California had become well known, the wooden side paddle-wheeler [*PMSSC California*] stopped in Panama to pick up a few passengers on route to San Francisco. But at Panama the ship instead found hundreds of gold-seekers waiting to board. They had made their way down the East Coast after hearing of the discovery at Sutter's Mill and crossed the Isthmus. Upon reaching San Francisco [February 28, 1849], all the passengers disembarked for the gold fields east of Sacramento. To the captain's disdain, so did most of the crew!" [14]

If the Panama route was the fastest way to the gold fields, it also offered the quickest route back to the eastern United States. To meet the demand, Pacific Mail Steamship Company had fourteen ships in service by 1851. These Panama steamers were driven by massive single-cylinder steam engines turning massive, thirty-foot diameter paddlewheels, supplemented by sails on two, three or four masts. Passengers in first and second class enjoyed well-ventilated, nicely appointed staterooms with access to public lounges. Steerage passengers slept in canvas bunks stacked three-high. [15]

Disembarking at Panama City – possibly wading ashore the final distance depending upon the tide - Captain Adams would have joined an all-too-familiar mule train twenty miles along narrow trails though virgin jungle and mangrove swamps to the divide, then proceeding through the swarming clouds of sand-flies and mosquitoes down the black, alligator -filled Chagres River in a large dugout canoe called a *bungo* to the Chagres estuary opening into the Caribbean. (Crossing this sixty-mile neck separating the American continents took about a week. The passage would be trimmed from days to hours with completion of a narrow-gauge railroad three years later.). At the port of Chagres, passengers boarded waiting ships for the voyage via Cuba to either New Orleans or east coast ports. In 1851, the clipper ship *Flying Cloud* sailed around the Horn from New York to San Francisco in a record eighty-nine days. The entire Panama route could be negotiated in about thirty-five days depending upon time in Panama waiting for passage. With completion of the Panama rail line, faster ships and better coordination between Atlantic and Pacific sailing schedules, the entire journey was reduced to about twenty-one days.

Disembarking in the bustling port of New Orleans, Captain Adams spent little time enjoying the cosmopolitan delta port, with its pungent mix of Spanish, French, Creole, Acadian and Anglo cultures. He cleared U.S. customs and secured passage on a Mississippi riverboat, while sweating, ebony-skinned African American slaves loaded and unloaded massive cotton bales and other items from the cavernous warehouses alongside the docks. In California, the few Africans or their descendants had surely faced discrimination, but they had been a couple thousand miles from the bonds of slavery. Here on the Mississippi, the slaves working the river boats "were able to participate in a river-linked black community which stretched from slave states to free ones, thereby not only gaining contact with new acquaintances but keeping track of previous ones, sometimes relatives, from whom they were separated. They were in a position to negotiate a degree of autonomy not offered to them in the fields...and-as with fictional Jim [in Mark Twain's novel, *The Adventures of Huckleberry Finn]*-to find an avenue to a more literal freedom." [16.] But they were still enslaved.

Like a young horse in spring, he could smell the barn and was anxious to finally get home. A week later, remembering the near tragedy of the steamboat accident on his return from the Mexican War, Captain Adams was glad to leave the boat at Alton, some fifteen miles upriver from St. Louis. Given the high number of riverboat fires, boiler explosions and miscellaneous sinkings, Alton was home to several insurance companies, earning the nickname "Insuranceville."[16.] Back in Illinois, only a few miles from Edwardsville, everything was familiar. He arrived home on October 12. He had been gone two-and-a-half years.

Captain Adams savored his reunion with Matilda, his daughters Mary and Alice, as well as meeting Sarah Jane, now age two, for the first time. He probably enjoyed being in the company of women, after years in the almost completely male population of the diggings. Whatever few women had been in the mining camps had worked the saloons or the back-alley cribs, offering quick pleasure to unwashed, drunken, and often diseased miners in return for a measure of their hard-worked flakes of gold. The Adams children listened wide-eyed to his tales of wagon trains, gold mines and ocean steamers. When he raised his intention to return to California with the entire family, Matilda neither enthused nor objected. Few pioneer women during the gold rush ever initiated the idea of making the trek to California. Rather, they acquiesced to their menfolk and hoped for the best. During the winter of 1851-1852, he busied himself putting affairs in order, selling his general store business and making his goodbyes around his hometown for the last time.

It may have been comforting to J. H. Adams, once back on the trail that spring of 1852, that everything seemed so familiar. True, the trail was more well defined by wagon wheel ruts. Wagon trains were even longer than three years before and now carried more families. The various native tribes were even more resentful of this incursion into ancestral lands. But the geography was the same. The same rivers and mountains had to be crossed. The same landmarks stood where that had been for millions of years. He knew what to expect.

Matilda Adams was pregnant again. She likely walked most of the first half of the journey, taking to the wagon only after walking became too uncomfortable. By the time they reached the Humboldt Sink, in high summer heat, her delivery was imminent. There in a tent pitched in that bleached boneyard of dashed dreams in the high desert, she gave birth to a son (another boy child, John Washington had died in childhood years before). They named the boy William and following the custom of recognizing someone of prominence- and with a good dash of ironic humor-appended the middle name of Humboldt. (As he named so many western features after someone he admired, John Fremont had named the Humboldt River after German naturalist Alexander von Humboldt. Humboldt, himself, never saw this particular example of hell on earth.)

Now numbering six, the Adams family settled in at Manhattan Creek, near Georgetown, where Allen Pomeroy, carrying the scar on his shin from the Indian attack, had staked out a claim for Captain Adams that had proved quite productive during his absence. But perhaps weary of mining and aware that the Mother Lode was not as generous with its golden bounty as it had been a couple years before, Captain Adams looked for a more suitable environment in which to raise his growing family. In spring they left the diggings and removed to the Great Central Valley before finally purchasing a ranch site in the fertile valley that opened from the lower reaches of San Francisco Bay, not far south from the first state capital of San Jose. There he would build a home and life for his family. And in this Valley of Heart's Delight, he would create his legend.

Notes:

1. Keith Heyer Meldahl, *Hard Road West–History and Geology along the Gold Rush Trail*, Chicago: The University of Chicago Press, 2007, p. 264.

2. "Old Hangtown," The Gold Rush Chronicles, http://goldrushchronicles.com>hangtown, retrieved Jan. 2, 2022.

3. "The True Story of Hangtown," *Sacramento Daily Union*, Vol. 11, No. 55, April 24, 1880, California Digital Newspaper Collection, University of California Riverside Center for Biographical Studies and Research, https://cdnc.urcr.edu, retrieved Jan. 11, 2022.

4. "Captain John H. Adams, a Mexican Veteran and a 49-er – An Adventurous Life," *San Jose Pioneer Press*, 1878.

5. Ibid.

6. https://www.auburn.ca.gov>Auburns-History.

7. David C. Antonucci, *Yours, Mine, Ours. An Explanitive History of the People and Environment of Lake Tahoe*, https://www.tahoefact.com>Yours-Mine-Ours-v10-e, p. 26, retrieved Jan. 20, 2022.

8. Ibid. p. 29.

9. "Drytown, Cal.," https:cali49.com>hwy49>drytown-cal, retrieved Jan. 13, 2022.

10. *Captain John H. Adams, a Mexican Veteran and a 49er-An Adventurous life*, op cit.

11. Alan Beilharz, "Legacy of the California Gold Rush," *Discover Coloma: A Teacher's Guide*, Gold Discovery

Park Association, https://www.marshallgold.com/, retrieved Jan. 2, 2022.

12. Simon Winchester, *Land*, New York: Harper Perennial, 2022, p. 379.

13. Kemble, John Haskell, "The Panama Route to the Pacific Coast, 1848-1869," *Pacific Historical Review*, Vol. 7, No. 1, University of California Press, 1938, pp. 1-13, https://doi.org/10.2307/3633844, retrieved Jan. 12, 2022.

14. "Pacific Mail Steamship Company," https://www.foundsf.org.title=Pacific_Mail_Steamship, retrieved Jan. 12, 2022.

15. "The Panama Route," University of California Press, https://publishing.cdlib.org>ucpressbooks>view, retrieved Jan. 12, 2022.

16. "African-Americans in the Mississippi River Valley 1857-1900," Northern Illinois University, https://digital.lib.niu.edu>twain>liberty, retrieved Jan. 12, 2022.

17. "Alton and the Mississippi River," *MCHS News*, Madison County Historical Society, Vol. 12, No. 5, September 2014, https://madcohistory.org>uploads-2019>2, retrieved Jan. 12, 2022.

Illustrations

OLD COURT HOUSE.

Original Madison County "Donation" Courthouse in Edwardsville, Illinois, in use 1825-57.

The building on the right is the county jail, site of the 1838 jailbreak in which young deputy John Hicks Adams captured the escaped prisoners and returned them to this jail.

Source: *History of Madison County Illinois, Edwardsville: W.R. Brink & Co., (1882)* Madison County Historical Society.

Voltigeur, Infantry, Dragoon, Artillery (campaign uniform) 1841-51, **Painting by Henry Alexander Ogden (1856-1936).**

Voltigeur was a French term for skirmish or sharpshooter units. During the Mexican War, Captain Adams's uniform would have had shoulder insignia of officer rank instead of chevrons on sleeve.

Source: Public Domain. Originally published in H.A. Ogden (illustrator), Lieut. Col. M.I. Ludington, and Brig. Gen. S.A. Holabird, *Uniforms of the Army of the United States Army, Washington D.C.: Office of the Quartermaster General of the U.S. Army, 1889.*

Lithography by G.H. Buek & Co., New York.

***Westport Landing (1937)*, Painting by William Henry Jackson (1843-1942).**

Missouri River steamboats unload wagons as pioneers make ready for the long trip west.

Source: *Scotts Bluff National Monument 280*, Courtesy National Parks Service.

HANGTOWN~1849, NOW PLACERVILLE, CALIF.

Placerville c. 1850.

A view of Hang Town (Old Dry Diggins/Placerville), showing the famous hanging tree to the left of the Empire building, rear center right.

Source: El Dorado County Historical Museum.

Portrait of Sheriff John Hicks Adams, c **1875.**

Source: Smith-Layton Archives at Sourisseau Academy for State and Local History, San Jose State University.

Portrait of Matilda Pomeroy Adams, **date unknown.**

Source: Courtesy Rebecca Pasquinelli Collection.

Engraving of Santa Clara County Courthouse & Jail 1876.

The building to the rear is the county jail.

Source: *1876 Thompson and West Atlas of Santa Clara County.* Smith-Layton Archives at the Sourisseau Academy for State and Local History, San Jose State University.

Portrait of Tiburcio Vasquez c. 1870.

The notorious *Californio bandido* was pursued relentlessly by Sheriff Adams.

Source: Smith-Layton Archives at the Sourisseau Academy for State and Local History, San Jose State University.

Portrait of Abdon Leiva, **date unknown.**

A member of the Vasquez gang, Leiva ultimately turned against Vasquez, who had seduced Leiva's wife.

Source: Smith-Layton Archives at the Sourisseau Academy for State and Local History, San Jose State University.

Gallows where Tiburcio Vasquez met his fate.

Source: Loryea Brothers photograph. Smith-Layton Archives at the Sourisseau Academy for State and Local History, San Jose State University.

SHERIFF'S OFFICE,

County of Santa Clara.

San Jose, March............1875.

To..

SIR.—Pursuant to the Statute in such cases you are hereby invited to be present at the execution of Tiburcio Vasquez, at the Jail of said County, in San Jose, on the 19th day of March, A. D. 1875, at 1:30 o'clock P. M.

J. H. ADAMS, Sheriff.

PRESENT AT JAIL ENTRANCE.   NOT TRANSFERABLE

FACSIMILE

Invitation to the execution of Tiburcio Vasquez issued by Sheriff Adams 1875.

Source: Smith-Layton Archives at the Sourisseau Academy for State and Local History, San Jose State University.

113

Portrait of Cornelius Finley.

Friend and mining partner, Finley accompanied Sheriff Adams to Arizona where they were both gunned down by the Celaya gang.

Source: Officer Memorial Page, U.S. Dept. of Justice, U.S. Marshal's office.

Portrait of Crawley P. Dake.

U.S. Marshal for Arizona Territory who deputized Adams and Finley shortly before they were ambushed and murdered.

Source: Wikimedia Commons.

Portraits of brothers Frank (right) and Tom McLaury.

Distant cousins of Cornelius Finley, the McLaury brothers were killed in the Gunfight at the O.K. Corral.

Source: Wikimedia Commons.

Portrait of Wyatt Earp.

In avenging his brother's murder, the famed gunfighter lawman also avenged the killing of John Hicks Adams and Cornelius Finley.

Source: Wikimedia Commons.

Chapter 5

Rancho Solis

"Ranches of Unknown extent, even to their owners...covered with vast herds of cattle and horses whose number also is generally unknown to the proprietors."

–Description of south Santa Clara Valley,
U.S. Census Bureau, 1850

Uvas Creek meanders some thirty miles from its origin on Loma Prieta Mountain, southward through a bucolic valley of the same name, before joining the Pajaro River south of present-day city of Gilroy as it flows on toward the Pacific Ocean. The Uvas (Spanish for "the grapes") Valley is one of the most scenic and serene areas of the Santa Clara Valley. Here Captain Adams brought his family in August 1853.

More than a thousand indigenous native Americans, the Amah Mutsun (Ohlone) tribe, had lived a bountiful, idyllic life in a village along the year-round, freshwater creek since from time before memory. Nature supplied ample game and fowl. Uvas Creek offered abundant trout, as well as ocean dwelling salmon and eels where it fed into the Pajaro River. The dense woodlands and well-drained soils yielded grapes, acorns, nuts and berries. Fish and shellfish were a day's walk across the Santa Cruz Mountains to the Pacific coast. Streamside willows were used in basket making.

The peaceful, centuries-old way of life ended abruptly for the Mutsun in the spring of 1776 with the arrival of Spanish explorers led by Captain Juan Bautista de Anza, on expedition through the Uvas Valley. (It is possible that the first contact was actually earlier, in 1774, when the Fernando Rivera-Palou expedition ventured north from Monterey on a scouting mission. Fernando Rivera y Moncada had been second in command to original California explorer Gaspar de Portola, who discovered San Francisco Bay and on a second expedition established the *Presidio* (fort) at Monterey. Rivera has largely been forgotten by history). Franciscan missionaries followed, establishing a string of missions in Alta California, including at nearby San Juan Bautista (1797) and Santa Cruz (1791). Within a generation, the native Americans had been removed to the missions, where they were forced to provide the unfamiliar labor necessary to maintain the missions while the Franciscans sought to baptize and Christianize them. In fact, many native Americans suffered from hardship and died of foreign illnesses in the shadow of what writer Elias Castillo called the "Cross of Thorns" and their population declined rapidly. [1]

The former soldiers at the Presidios of Monterey and San Francisco were few and poorly paid. However, they were able to obtain land licenses from the King of Spain. These became the vast *ranchos* of early California. For their part, the Franciscan missionaries also tried to acquire as much land for the missions as possible, inevitably coming into conflict with the land-holding *dons.* The Spanish overlords of Alta (Upper) California were anxious to populate this outpost of empire as a hedge against Russian and English encroachment from the northwest. The process was simple: file a petition and submit a crude map called a *diseno,* often using trees, rock outcroppings or creeks as boundary markers. Petitions ranged from the size of a house to more than 48,000 acres.

Soldiers and their families from the Mission Dolores at Yerba Buena (later San Francisco) and the Presidio in Monterey were encouraged to move closer to Santa Clara Mission. The pueblo of San Jose de Guadalupe was established in 1777 and in 1782 the Spanish government partitioned Mission Santa Clara land to nine settlers close to San Jose. In 1803, the Spanish Viceroy granted the 8,875-acre (two Leagues) Rancho Las Animas, including land along the Uvas Creek, to Jose Mariano Castro, a former soldier at Monterey and son of Joaquin Isidro Castro who had been a member of the original de Anza Expedition and a founder of San Jose.

Following Mexican independence from Spain in 1821, and the secularization of the mission properties in 1833, Mexico continued the land grant practice, in part as a buffer against foreigners, now including Anglos from the United States. The Secularization Act was designed to return most of the mission properties to the indigenous peoples, but in fact most was offered to *Californios* (Mexicans of Spanish descent born in California). In 1827 a former soldier named Joaquin Solis applied for his own land grant along the Uvas. When his application failed, he led a short-lived rebellion against the government before being deported to Mexico. Meanwhile, Jose Mariano Castro had died in 1828. It took until 1835 for his widow, Josefa Romero de Castro, and their eight children to secure their inheritance. (One section of their vast property was sold to Martin Murphy, the pioneer who had first brought wagons over the Sierra Nevada in 1844, and, as an Irish Catholic, was able to obtain Mexican citizenship and Mexican land grants in the Santa Clara Valley.) The land in the Uvas Valley continued to be known as Rancho Solis.

The first naturalized English-speaking settler in all of Alta California had been Scottish-born sailor, John Cameron, who had changed his surname to Gilroy, his mother's maiden name. He had been on board the British merchantman *Isaac Todd*, enroute to seize the American trading post at Astoria, Oregon during the War of 1812. In 1814, the ship put in at the Mexican port of Monterey in Alta California to resupply and Gilroy either was sent ashore to recover from scurvy or jumped ship. He converted to Catholicism, was baptized Juan Bautista Gilroy at the mission in Monterey and eventually found work as a cooper, making barrels used for the export of cattle hides and tallow. By 1821 Gilroy had married Maria Clara, the daughter of Igancio Ortega, *ranchero* of the 13,000-acre Rancho San Ysidro. Gilroy's wife inherited a third of the rancho in 1833. (The property would be later patented to husband John Gilroy under U.S. property law in 1867). Gilroy raised cattle and made soap on Rancho San Ysidro. A town grew up around the village of San Ysidro and Gilroy was appointed *alcalde* (mayor) and *juez de paz* (justice of the peace) in 1846.[2] Originally located near the opening to the Pacheco Pass that led east through the Gabilan Mountains to the Great Central Valley, flood-prone San Ysidro eventually gave way to a newer Gilroy farther west. By 1850, Gilroy was a stagecoach stop and mail station along *El Camino Real*, the original mission highway through Alta California and the road connecting San Jose and Monterey.

At mid-century with the gold rush and U.S. annexation and statehood, California's equilibrium changed forever almost overnight. Although the original Mexican land ownership was supposed to be recognized by U.S. law, with this flood of Anglo Americans, the original Mexican land grant license holders faced enormous difficulty, delays and expense - and prejudice - trying to validate their titles in American courts. Many *Californios* sold their properties for whatever they could get, lost their land to squatters, or were dispossessed in title hearings. The days of the *ranchos* had passed. With profits from gold mining, Captain Adams bought a farm section of Rancho Solis from the widow of Mariano Castro, though the terms are unknown. (The original Mexican land grants did not convey title but rather license to occupy and use tracts of land. After California statehood, Congress enacted legislation which allowed licensees or their successors to register the land through a process of survey and approval on a first-registered, first-approved basis and receive title. In 1875, the U.S. Supreme Court upheld the process in *Miller et al. v. Dale et al.,* which ruled that a second licensee of Rancho Solis had completed the process first and owned title and thus could not be evicted. By then, Adams had long-since subdivided the rancho at a profit and ultimately divested his interest in the property and moved to San Jose.)[3]

124

Like the Spaniards and Mexicans before them, these new settlers in California, including Captain Adams, raised livestock and raised grain crops. Some of his neighbors began planting orchards and experimenting with vineyards. Native grapes (*vitus californica*) had been flourishing wild when the Spaniards arrived, and the mission fathers had cultivated grapes for the sacramental wines and mission use. Mission grapes would later be replaced by more palatable imported varieties. By the 1850s, the Santa Clara Valley was well on its way to becoming one of the premier wine-making regions of the state. Timber began to be harvested for lumber from the slopes of Mount Madonna in the Santa Cruz coastal range, just west of the Adams ranch.

In 1859, Adams donated part of his land for the establishment of a one room schoolhouse for local children on the site of the former Mutsun/Ohlone village along Uvas Creek. Adams School served as a community gathering place for social events, Sunday School activities and civic engagement for residents of the rural area, some ten miles from Gilroy proper. Over the years, at least two school structures stood there. The first school burned around 1915. Rebuilt, the school continued in operation until another fire, possibly arson, destroyed it in 1956 when the school closed permanently. The site is now incorporated into Chictactac -Adams Heritage

County Park. Generations of children used the ancient sandstone outcroppings, pock-marked with Indian grinding holes, and illustrated with petroglyphs, as their playground, and Uvas Creek as their swimming hole. Children arriving for school in the morning could see deer, bear and mountain lion tracks near the front door.

A plaque, erected by the historical society E Clampus Vitus on the former Adams School site reads:

CHITACTAC-ADAMS HERITAGE COUNTY PARK

CHITACTAC

FOR OVER 3,000 YEARS THIS AREA AROUND THE UVAS CREEK DRAINAGE SUPPORTED LARGE POPULATIONS OF ANCESTRAL OHLONE PEOPLE. THIS LOCATION IS BELIEVED TO BE THE ETHNOHISTORIC VILLAGE OF CHITACTAC. THE FIRST EUROPEAN CONTACT WITH THIS MAJOR VILLAGE MAY HAVE OCCURRED IN NOVEMBER 1774 DURING THE RIVERA-PALOU EXPEDITION

ADAMS SCHOOL HOUSE

IN 1859 JOHN HICKS ADAMS, 'AN OLD AND EXPERIENCED MINER,' FUTURE POLITICIAN AND SHERIFF DONATED THIS PROPERTY TO THE ADAMS SCHOOL DISTRICT FOR A SCHOOLHOUSE. RECORDS ARE VAGUE BUT AT LEAST TWO SCHOOLS WERE BUILT ON THE SITE WITH THE LAST ONE BEING BURNED DOWN IN 1956[4]

By 1861, Adams abandoned farming and entered local politics. Santa Clara County had been administered by a Court of Sessions until 1852, when it reorganized under a Board of Supervisors. John Hicks Adams was elected as a Santa Clara County Supervisor for Gilroy and Almaden Townships from October 1861 to November 1862. The large *ranchos* were being carved up into farm plots. Captain Adams had sold part of his holdings to a pair of brothers from Pennsylvania, Speer and D.C. Riddell. Speer Riddell had come to California in 1852 and established himself in San Francisco banking. His brother followed in 1857. In 1861, the brothers purchased 865 acres in the Uvas Valley including part of the former Rancho Solis, for cattle ranching, sowing the hillsides with wheat or barley hay and using the flat valley floor for stone fruits such as Bartlett pears, apricots and French prunes. Speer Ridell eventually became president of the San Bernardino Borax Mining Company. D.C. Riddell later retired in Gilroy as the local Wells Fargo agent.[5] Gilroy was a rapidly growing community already lobbying for a railroad connection, but Almaden was the barely populated site of the New Almaden Quicksilver Mine. Mercury from the mine was used in the processing of gold. This would become the stage of Captain Adams's most dramatic exploit within a couple of years. He was serving a second elected term as Supervisor in February 1864, when County Sheriff James Faris Kennedy suddenly died.

Faris Kennedy had come to California in 1850 as an agent of Commodore Stockton to sell a large tract of land between the towns of San Jose and Santa Clara. He set himself up as a rancher near Los Gatos in the Santa Cruz Mountains foothills and became well known as an orchardist and breeder of fine running and trotting racehorses. Active in the Republican Party, in 1859 he had been the candidate for lieutenant governor of California on the ticket with Leland Stanford. He had been elected sheriff of Santa Clara County in 1863.[6]

Captain Adams had already decided to run for County Sheriff and had defeated William Aram by a four-to three margin, when the incumbent Sheriff Kennedy died. As Sheriff-elect he was appointed to finish out the final month of Kennedy's term, before his own term began. Although still known unofficially as "Captain Adams", the following narrative will use "Sheriff" as a more exact title. As he stepped forward to keep the peace in Santa Clara County during the turbulence of the Civil War, he also was stepping into the history of law enforcement in the Old West.

Notes:

1. Elias Castillo, *A Cross of Thorns*, Fresno, CA: Linden Publishing, Inc. 2015.

2. "A Brief History of Gilroy," City of Gilroy, California, https://www.cityofgilroy.org>Hitory-of-Gilroy, retrieved Jan. 18, 2022.

3. "Miller v. Dale 92 U.S. 473 (1875)," https://supreme.justia.com>cases>federal, retrieved Feb. 8, 2022.

4. Chitactac-Adams Heritage County Park, plaque, Mountain Charlie Chapter No. 1850, E Clampus Vitus, dedicated June, 12, 1993.

5. *Pen Pictures from the Garden of the World or Santa Clara County, California, Illustrated*, H.S. Foote, ed., Chicago: The Lewis Publishing Co., 1888, pp. 393-394, transcribed by Kathy Sedler.

6. J.M. Guinn, *History of the State of California & Biographical Record of Coast Counties, California*, Chicago: The Chapman Publishing Co., 1904, pp. 1107-1108, transcribed by Marilyn R. Pankey, Mar. 24, 2016.

Chapter 6

Partisans and Pistols

"It is not my intention to be captured."

–Rufus Henry Ingram

Like his father before him, John Hicks Adams was now a county sheriff and he seemed well-suited for the role. Now in his early forties, he was at full strength and maturity. At no more than medium height, there was no mistaking the muscularity under his black frock coat, set off by white shirt and tie. The tail of his coat hid the shine on the seat of his pants from long hours in the saddle and when pulled back exposed the pistol nestled in a worn leather holster, heavy yet comfortable against his hip. His vest displayed a pocket watch and chain and the shield-shaped sheriff's badge. He wore his hair neither short nor long like the fashion-conscious Bill Hickok or William F. Cody, but simply combed back from a receding hairline. He wore a beard and moustachios in a style of the times (suspiciously jet black), without sideburns and trimmed before it fell too far below his chin. His countenance was open and friendly, but his gaze mirrored an inner determination. Adams still retained-unofficially-his Army officer rank of Captain and his no-nonsense authority was often sufficient to bring the lesser miscreants, drunks, gamblers and vagrants, to heel. For the more serious outlaws, such as horse thieves, stage robbers and murderers, there was mother Colt and her six children in the gun belt around his waist.

With statehood, law enforcement in California matured. The iconic duel at high noon in the middle of the street between the good and the bad almost never happened. Routine arrests of the drunk and disorderly were the norm; climactic shoot outs between posses and surrounded outlaw gangs were the exception. A functioning judicial system evolved to replace the vigilante justice and lynching common in the mining camps. From 1850 to 1879, district and county courts in California handled felony cases, such as murder, robbery or burglary (Superior courts evolved in 1880 and appellate courts only after 1904). Convicted felons were sent to state prison, usually a brig anchored in San Francisco Bay before construction of the San Quentin stone cell block in 1854. Condemned men were executed by hanging in the yard of the local county jail or courthouse. Each county elected a sheriff for a two-year term. He was normally assisted by an undersheriff and any number of deputies. Counties were divided into townships, each having a justice of the peace and an elected constable. Larger cities, such as San Francisco, also had a police department headed by a chief or city marshal. California also had two United States marshals, responsible for enforcing federal law.[1]

Following the conclusion of the Mexican War and the annexation of California, the dusty *pueblo* of San Jose, at the south end of San Francisco Bay, was governed by a town council, *or ayuntamiento.* At the first constitutional convention prior to statehood in Monterey in September 1849, delegates from San Jose lobbied successfully for San Jose to become the first capital of the new state. But lawmakers bemoaned the isolation and lack of amenities available in San Jose and within two years voted to move the state capital north to Vallejo. By 1850, San Jose had a population of 4,000 inhabitants, although many of its young men had abandoned the city during the gold rush. Local government operated out of an adobe building called a *juzgado,* serving as court, jail and mayor's office. Following the formation of Santa Clara County in April 1851, several buildings served as the county courthouse. In 1866, partly to lure the state capital back to San Jose, locals erected a prestigious, neo-classical courthouse with stately columns and a solid copper dome on North First Street, across from a public park.[2.] Although the state capital never returned to San Jose, the courthouse anchored county government and the adjacent jail was the domain of Sheriff Adams for many years.

In 1992, during the earthquake restoration effort of the old courthouse, engineers and construction workers made an interesting discovery. According to *the Mercury News* on July 20, 1992, "Deep in the bowels of the 124- year-old Santa Clara County Courthouse are two forgotten high-security jail cells". The cell, with four-inch-thick double safety doors and steel ceilings were heavy duty and primitive. Though gas outlets indicated heat was available, there were no plumbing facilities...Within the cells, workers found numerous old documents including some Mexican era hand drawn boundary maps." [3]

As the seat of county government, San Jose continued slow but steady growth. A mild climate and fertile soil created an agricultural bonanza. San Jose became known as the *Garden City* -nestled in the *Valley of Heart's Delight.* [4]

Candidates for County sheriff and other positions ran indicating their political party affiliation and Adams campaigned as a Republican, the party of Abraham Lincoln. It is not clear whether his political preference was from deeply held ideology or out of respect for his fellow Illinoian, now the president. But Adams's pro-Lincoln stance on slavery and other issues influenced his performance as sheriff, particularly as those same issues--and that same president—embroiled the nation in tragic civil war.

Californians were very interested in following the news as the national debate over slavery gained momentum. Many were originally from the southern and midwestern states or territories where the slavery issue was unsettled. And, of course, many immigrants who had arrived during the gold rush or shortly afterward, still had family in the east. The California Constitutional Convention had unanimously approved abolition and free state status, although that viewpoint was not universally shared by the population.

In general, northern California leaned pro-Union during the late 1850s, with pockets of southern sympathizers and so-called secessionists in San Joaquin, Santa Clara, Monterey and San Francisco counties while secessionists held a majority viewpoint in southern California. In 1853, Secretary of War Jefferson Davis (later President of the Confederacy) pushed for a rail link to California along a southern route, obviously favoring southern interests. In 1856, James Gadsden, who had negotiated the annexation of Arizona and New Mexico, called for splitting California into two states, the southern California state to trade rice, cotton and sugar with southern states by a rail line- built by slave labor - from New Orleans to Los Angeles. He also advocated resettling some 2,000 African

American slaves in southern California. As early as 1823, Gadsden had organized the resettlement of Seminole Indians from Florida and Georgia, part of the forced relocation of some 60,000 Native Americans from nine states that became known as the *Trail of Tears.* The Pico Act of 1859 included a provision to make southern California a slave-owning part of Colorado Territory, a measure that in fact passed the California legislature and was approved by Governor John B. Weller before fractures among factions of Democrats in the House of Representatives doomed the measure to congressional failure. California was far from immune from the vitriol and violence gripping the nation. [5]

Though a minority political party in California, the Republicans managed to gain a plurality over a divided Democratic party and win the state for Lincoln in 1860. Most volunteer companies of California militia had been disbanded due to divided loyalties, but at the onset of war new units were formed, often under the direction of county sheriffs. Among the thirteen such units formed in Santa Clara County was the Gilroy Guard, Company E, 5th Infantry Regiment, 2nd Brigade, under John Hicks Adams, as captain. As the secession crisis worsened and frustrated by the failure of the various partition schemes, southern secessionists and many *Californios,* formed their own militia units, including the Los Angeles Mounted

136

Rifles. As the firing on Fort Sumter began the cascade of seceding southern states, Albert Sydney Johnston, Commander of the U.S. Army Department of the Pacific, a southern sympathizer but not pro-secession, rejected a proposed plan for a Pacific Republic of California and Oregon. Then, after refusing to surrender federal installations at San Francisco and Benicia, he nevertheless resigned and led members of the Los Angeles Mounted Rifles across New Mexico to Texas, where he joined the Confederate army and became a noted general. The Mounted Rifles militia founder, Tomas Sanchez, also had founded the Los Angeles Police Department. Staying behind during the Civil War, Sanchez became the first Mexican American Los Angeles County Sheriff, reelected for seven years. Adams would serve for ten. Throughout California, secessionist armed activity was blunted by federal troops and local Home Guard units including one in Santa Clara County organized by Captain Adams.[6]

As the cannons barked at Bull Run and the Confederates enjoyed early success, secession of southern California seemed a distinct possibility. To counter public support for secession, federal authorities clamped down on newspapers suspected of being in sympathy with the southern cause. In Placerville, *The El Dorado Republican* had been supplanted by the *Mountain Democrat*, which was denied postal privileges during the war.

A competing pro-Union paper, The *Placerville Republican* was edited by Thomas Fitch who was known as the "Silver Tongued Orator of the Pacific" for his rousing support of the boys in blue. (Fitch later became a lawyer and defended, among others, Brigham Young in the Mormon polygamy case and the Earp brothers along with Doc Holliday for murdering three outlaws at the O.K. Corral-the Old West's most infamous gunfight with an eerie coincidence to the story of John Hicks Adams.) [7]

Both the Union and Confederacy coveted California's gold deposits. And men on both sides volunteered for military service. Confederate volunteers generally joined regiments in Texas. Approximately 17,000 men volunteered for Union service, filling several regiments and battalions of cavalry and infantry. Many California troopers saw action in the east, attached to other states' units while other California units remained in-state securing the borders, defending against native tribes and addressing the large number of southern sympathizers. [8]

Not only was the Confederacy interested in the gold resources, but California also offered another resource the Confederacy desperately needed: an open harbor along the southern California coast, unaffected by the Union Blockade. [9] This dual desire for nuggets and a navy opened an interesting chapter in California's role in the Civil War, as well as becoming the starting point for what became Sheriff Adams's most well-known and courageous exploit.

The Confederacy had long hoped for support from Britain or France or, at least, some iron-clad sailing vessels being developed in Europe. But both Britain and France warily guarded their new maritime technology and refused. As a fallback, Confederate President Jefferson Davis offered commissions to privateers, as in Elizabethan times, to outfit their own ships with guns and prey on Union shipping. One young adventurer named Ashbury Harpending outfitted the schooner *J.M. Chapman* in a two-fold plot to raid Pacific Mail Steamship Company shipping along the Pacific coast and to salvage some two million dollars in gold from the sunken *S.S. Golden Gate,* off the coast of Mexico. Booty and salvaged gold would be sent to support the Confederacy. All this secessionist piracy needed was a crew.

The first to sign on for this action was a middle-aged rancher and widower from the Watsonville area along the Pajaro River named Tom Poole. Poole was an ardent Democrat and a member of a semi-secret organization of secessionists called Knights of the Golden Circle. The Knights of the Golden Circle aimed to overthrow the weak Mexican government and establish a slave state in its stead. The society numbered in the thousands but met clandestinely in cells throughout the state using secret signs and passwords. Members included many ranchers and prominent San Jose businessmen. In addition to being an ardent *sesesh man*, as secessionists were called, or *Copperhead (*for removing the words *United States of America* from a coin worn as a badge, leaving only the engraved head showing*),* Poole held a grudge against the government of California. In 1858, as undersheriff of Monterey County, Poole had ignored a reprieve notice from Governor Weller and executed a convicted murderer, justifying his actions by a misspelled name on the reprieve. A nasty exchange between the Governor and Poole ensued and Poole lost his job. Nevertheless, after so many violent murders in the community, many local residents still supported him. Removed from his position, Poole wandered from Monterey to San Francisco where he met Ashbury Harpending at a Knights of the Golden Circle meeting. Poole was a willing recruit. On the morning of March 15, 1863, the small crew of would-be privateers on board the *J.M. Chapman* in San Francisco Bay were awakened to see the U.S. sloop of war *U.S.S. Cyane* bearing down on them, forward guns primed, followed by a small flotilla of boats carrying federal customs and revenue officers and San Francisco police. Game over before setting sail.

Poole and the others were charged with treason and imprisoned on Alcatraz, the former Spanish prison island in the middle of the numbingly cold water and strong currents of San Francisco Bay, before being released months later after pledging allegiance to the Union. Poole had no intention of keeping the oath. He joined the San Jose Chapter of the Knights of the Golden Circle, which alternated its secret meetings between one location in Arroyo Hondo, east of San Jose and the other in the foothills to the west of the city. There Poole met an enigmatic young man who introduced himself as Rufus Henry Ingram, a captain in the Confederate Army who had ridden with the notorious William Quantrill's Raiders. Quantrill's raiders had terrorized the Kansas -Missouri border region in response to regional occupation by federal troops. He had led a devastating surgical strike against Union warehouses- and civilians in Lawrence, Kansas, burning and killing with abandon. The plunder was then sold to finance the southern cause. [10]

Rufus Ingram proposed assembling a unit of men to return to the east and fight for the Confederacy as regular troops. He may have been as he presented himself, though he showed his recruits no proof of identity. On the other hand, his profile may have been a composite by later historians or journalists, drawn from the military records of a several men, none of whom exactly match Confederate muster roll records, documentation of Quantrill's Raiders, or any of the other details of Ingram's back-story. The time frame does coincide with the summer recruitment efforts in Missouri by Confederate General Sterling Price (who had been commanding general in New Mexico during the Mexican War). And because Ingram simply disappears into history at the end of this misadventure, we will likely never know who he really was. Nonetheless, several men eagerly accepted this charismatic figure and agreed to enlist in Ingram's Partisan Rangers. Enlistees included his brother John Ingram; Tom Poole; brothers John and Wallace Clendenning; John Creal Bouldware, a carpenter; James Wilson, a young blacksmith from Missouri; Henry Jarboe; Joseph Gamble; Washington Jordan; John Gately and George Cross, a well-known pioneer associate of John Fremont and a successful gold miner. They would be later joined by young Missourian Alban Glasby and Jim Grant, a known killer and horse thief, and the only true outlaw of the Partisan Rangers.

During 1864, according to local historian Phil Reader, "Confederate guerillas bivouacked and trained in the rugged, redwood-crested Loma Prieta area, west of San Jose. Nearby ranchers, in allegiance with their cause, sheltered them from the prying eyes of the local Union militia unit known as the

Butler Guards, and the almost inaccessible terrain allowed them to move almost unnoticed in and out of their camp."[11] In the east foothills a rancher named Preston Hodges sheltered the band near his ranch in Arroyo Hondo. Here ingram formulated his plan to finance the group's long return trip to the south: intercept the gold and silver shipment from the Comstock Lode in Nevada on its way to Sacramento. He rationalized that since it was money destined to support the Union war effort and as they were legitimate Confederate soldiers – which they were not – it was fair game.

Meanwhile in San Jose, there was a new sheriff in town. Shortly after being sworn in as county sheriff, Adams became suspicious of the nightly activities of the Copperheads. With help of an informer, he and his equally stalwart undersheriff R.B. Hall discovered the guerilla lair at Loma Prieta Mountain. During a late-night stake-out of the hideout, prone in hiding, Hall recognized several prominent men from San Jose among the Knights members and overheard the full plan to raise money to support a Confederate military unit. By accident, Hall's pistol discharged, scattering the assembly in all directions, as they fled by horseback in fear of being identified.

To the by-the-book Sheriff Adams, the meeting technically had not been illegal. Still the sheriff was on high alert, concerned that a raid, like in Lawrence, Kansas, might be planned for San Jose.

In May, Ingram abandoned any plan to loot San Jose, instead reverting to the original idea of robbing a Wells Fargo stagecoach. Jim Grant and James Wilson were sent to Placerville on a reconnaissance mission to learn about the silver shipments. After the drunken Grant nearly disclosed the plans, the mission was aborted and Grant was cashiered from the group, but not before a couple of altercations with other group members, rumors of which made their way to the sheriff's office. Adams doubled the guard in San Jose, expecting trouble. Instead, Captain Ingram doubled down on the Placerville bullion heist.

On June 21, six of the Partisan Rangers: Ingram, Poole, George Baker, John Bouldware, John Clendenning and Al Glasby began the long ride across central California to the gold country, eventually spending the night at Somerset House, thirteen miles south of Placerville.

Western history writer John Boessenecker writes, "The Placerville toll road over the Sierra was by then one of the most heavily used highways in California. By day a continuous string of teams stretched from Placerville to Lake Tahoe, carrying freight to Virginia City and other Nevada mining camps. …The six-horse Concord coaches of the Pioneer Stage

144

Company carried much of the silver bullion across from the Comstock, treasure which helped greatly to finance the Union's war effort. Few but the Pioneer stages traveled the road after nightfall." [12]

The plan, as the band crouched behind boulders near a sharp bend in the road about eleven miles from Placerville, in the twilight of June 30, was to intercept the stagecoach, remove the treasure and bury it for later retrieval, before scattering to the west and regrouping in San Jose. Much later they would return to retrieve the cache and launder the money in San Francisco. Captain Ingram ordered no shooting unless in self-defense. This was a military operation; the fight was not with civilians. He had prepared an official-sounding receipt for the stolen wealth, referring to themselves as soldiers of the Confederate Army:

June 1864

This is to certify that I have received from Wells Fargo & Co. the sum of $_____ cash, for the purpose of outfitting recruits in California for the Confederate States Army.

/s/ R. Henry Ingram
Captain
Commanding Co., C.S.A.

At dusk, a pair of Pioneer Stage Line coaches, traveling in tandem a few minutes apart on their way to Sacramento with more than $40,000 in bullion, rounded the bend, the drivers reining back on the descent. Ingram stepped into the road and leveled his shotgun at the lead coach driver, Ned Blair. Poole grabbed the bridle of the lead horse to steady it. Ingram ordered Blair to throw down the strong box. "Come and get it" snarled the driver. Suddenly the second coach arrived. Surprised, Ingram now aimed his weapon at driver Charley Watson and ordered him to throw down the bullion he carried on the second stage. A passenger named McDougall, a Virginia City policeman, leaned out the coach window and fired a shot harmlessly into the night. But the retort spooked the first team of horses and they charged away down the road. Ingram addressed the passengers in the second coach: "Gentlemen, (there were also three women) I will tell you who we are. We are not robbers, but a company of Confederate soldiers. Don't act foolish. We don't want anything of the passengers. All we want is Wells, Fargo and Company's treasure to assist us to recruit for the Confederate Army." A seventeen-year-old girl engaged Al Glasby in conversation long enough to later be able to identify the masked bandit's voice if not his face (she was never called to testify). The passengers were not robbed, and the stagecoach was allowed to follow its sister coach down the

146

road. The partisans stashed the double load of coins and bullion in a nearby ravine, thinking it would be some time before the coaches would arrive in Placerville and a posse formed. In ingram's careful planning he had not considered the existence of a telegraph line at a roadhouse stop not far from the robbery site which became known as Bullion Bend. By the time the coaches reached Placerville after midnight, Sheriff William Rogers was already organizing a citizen posse along with deputies John Van Eaton, Joseph Staples and Constable George Ranney. As dawn broke, the lawmen had picked up the outlaw trail and followed it back to Pleasant Valley and Somerset House.[13]

Deputy Van Eaton returned to gather the rest of the posse, while Staples and Ranney approached the hotel. The partisans had ordered breakfast then retired to a bedroom to nap after riding all night. Made aware of the outlaws' presence by proprietress Maria Reynolds, Constable Ranney entered the bedroom, then seeing the partisans reach for their guns he quickly ducked back out. As he did, he passed Deputy Staples running in with a shotgun. From the bed, Ingram, Bouldware and Glasby all opened fire. Stumbling from the impact of multiple wounds, Staples fired the shotgun hitting Poole full in the face with buckshot. As Staples died on the porch, Ranney bolted for cover outside. The guerillas followed, pistols spewing lead at the retreating lawman. He collapsed in a nearby ravine, saying "I'm killed, don't fire anymore." A distraught Maria Reynolds prevented the partisans from administering a *coup de grace.* Instead, the partisans relieved the lawmen of coins and watches, gathered up the six guns and hurriedly left, leaving Tom Poole, his left cheek blown away, bleeding on the bed.[14]

Undersheriff Jim Hume reached the Somerset House hours later and found the corpse of his friend Joe Staples, the wounded Tom Poole and the riddled body of Constable Ranney, amazingly still alive. Hume was accompanied by Dr. H.W.A. Worthen whose apparent familiarity in treating gunshot wounds saved the lives of both Ranney and Poole. Poole was incarcerated in Placerville. From his jail cell he confessed to the robbery, named his fellow gang members, and indicated their plans to stage a raid in San Jose.

Meanwhile, the five outlaws were hightailing it across the state, back to the relative protection of Santa Clara County. Enroute one evening, the gang was surprised at their campsite by the approach of mounted riders. Thinking them to be a posse in pursuit, they scattered into the night, leaving behind their horses and even a looted bar of bullion. It would be a very long walk back to San Jose. The night riders proved not to be a posse, but rather horse thieves known as the Mason - Henry

148

Gang, looking to use the same rustler's roost for the night. Sheriff Adams would soon have to deal with them as well.

Alerted that the Ingram Gang was headed back to his jurisdiction, Adams moved to protect his turf and arrest the partisans for extradition back to El Dorado County. A suspicious rancher named Edward Hill reported to Sheriff Adams that five men had spent the night in one of his outbuildings and talked of robbing the stagecoach carrying the payroll to the New Almaden Mines, a few miles west of San Jose.

Sheriff Adams knew the New Almaden Mines area well. He had represented the district as a County Supervisor. The name Almaden was taken from the Arabic words for mines in Spain, *al maden.* Local Indians had used the red cinnabar powder for body decoration long before its industrial use was discovered. Because mercury when distilled, can attract other metals, the liquid metal was worth millions of dollars in the gold recovery process. By the 1860s, thousands of pounds of ore were being brought to the surface by Cornish, Mexican or Chilean miners each day. Six furnaces were in continuous operation. Thousands of dollars' worth of quicksilver were recovered from pools underneath the furnaces. The company prospered but the miners suffered greatly from vapors causing mercury poisoning.[15.] The miners lived in communities called

Spanishtown or English Camp on the hills surrounding the mine openings, but there were few buildings in the Almaden Valley and Sheriff Adams's ten-man posse found the Hill ranch easily.

The lawmen surrounded the ranch house, and heavily armed with pistols, rifles and shotguns, crouched in the brush. Characteristically, Sheriff Adams strode forward, authoritatively calling out "Come out and deliver yourselves up." The partisans spilled from the door, six guns blazing in each hand. In the first fusillade, Deputy Sheriff J.H.Brownlee was wounded twice in the leg. Outlaw John Clendenning's gunshot found its mark square on Sheriff Adams's chest. As the sheriff staggered from the impact, he brought up his own shotgun, loaded with "buck and ball," round shot designed for maximum lethal effect straight at the target plus smaller buckshot pellets that fanned out for collateral carnage. The shotgun blast peppered Clendenning's back as he scrambled over a fence to get away. Sheriff Adams, after a moment of shock, straightened up wincing in pain, wounded only slightly as the ball had struck his pocket watch and glanced off, only nicking his skin and bruising his ribs. The black powder used in the outlaw's cap and ball percussion pistol had produced a less forceful blast. The image of the burly lawman standing firm and resolute against a hail of gunfire would remain his legacy.

The other outlaws and deputies continued firing. Young Al Glasby was wounded, and his clothing pierced by seven bullets before he surrendered. Afraid of facing the hangman's noose, Glasby would turn states-evidence and testify before the El Dorado County grand jury against all his former fellow gang members. After an exchange of lead with Deputy Sheriff G.W. Reynolds and A. Bowman, outlaw John Bouldware was chased by Bowman and dropped by a shotgun blast. He expired after a final struggle. Clendenning was found dying among the willows nearby. The deputies recovered the watch he had taken from the slain Joe Staples at Somerset House. Taken by wagon to the jail in San Jose, Cllendenning made a full confession before dying the next morning. In the blue haze of gunsmoke, Rufus Ingham and George Baker had managed to escape, leaving no trail. Stories circulated that Ingram found his way out of California by means of a clandestine southern underground railroad and via Mexico returned to Texas to rejoin the Confederate Army during the waning months of the war. There is no evidence of this either way. Whether by choice or by chance, the gentlemanly, self-styled Confederate officer turned stagecoach robber simply evaporates into the obscurity of time.

Sheriff Adams, and Placerville lawmen Jim Hume and John Van Eaton, backed by four companies of Union soldiers, made a fast sweep through the Santa Cruz Mountains mopping up the remnants of the Ingram Partisan Rangers. Undersheriff Hall tracked down Jim Grant to a rendezvous in nearby Los Gatos with a woman named Katie Kincade, where he wounded and arrested Grant. Grant was convicted of larceny and sentenced to San Quentin prison. Jim Wilson was arrested at the Seven Mile House on the Monterey Road and Washington Jordan was captured in a billiard saloon at Half Moon Bay, on the San Mateo County coast. Preston Hodges, who had harbored the band, was convicted of murder in the second degree as an accomplice, but the conviction was overturned on appeal that the trial should have been in Santa Clara instead of El Dorado County. In 1865, Hodges and three others were indicted in Santa Clara County for murder and treason though five others were released for lack of evidence, or because only federal courts could hear cases of treason. That left Tom Poole the last man remaining in jail. Despite a groundswell of support for clemency, Governor Frederick Low rejected his plea, as Poole had rejected the reprieve of a convicted man in Monterey County years earlier. On September 29, 1865, Tom Poole dropped through the trap of the Placerville gallows, mystified to the end that he hadn't been treated as a Confederate prisoner of war, but rather as a common criminal. [16.]

The Civil War had ended with Lee's surrender at Appomattox. Lincoln had been assassinated and the freed slaves faced uncertainty during the period of Reconstruction. The war-weary nation tried to get on with life, binding up the wounds from the terrible conflict. But some wounds wouldn't heal. With the demise of the Ingram Gang, Sheriff Adams turned his attention to another renegade gang of Confederate partisans, the Mason-Henry Gang.

The Mason-Henry Gang was led by a pair of young southern sympathizers Tom McCauley (who went by the name James Henry) and John Mason (who sometimes used the alias John J. Monroe). The pair had been under the influence of Judge George Belt, a wealthy Stockton, California arch-secessionist, originally from Tennessee. Belt had armed and outfitted several partisan groups. Their guerilla tactics were hoped to hasten the establishment of a separate Pacific Republic. But as General Sherman swept through Georgia and into the Carolinas, and Robert E. Lee's Army of Virginia was pushed back toward Richmond, the tide of war had clearly turned. The Mason-Henry gang quickly deteriorated into a savage band of ruthless thieves and murderers. Yet, by calling themselves Confederate soldiers, they retained support among

California Copperheads as they preyed upon stagecoaches, ranches, and known abolitionists or Union supporters from the San Joaquin Valley up through Monterey, Santa Cruz and Santa Clara Counties.

From a spree of robbery and killings in the Central Valley, the gang rode over the Pacheco Pass and went to ground near the old Tom Poole hideout above the village of Corralitos on the Santa Cruz coast-side slopes of Loma Prieta Mountain. Now in his jurisdiction, Sheriff Adams pursued the gang with two companies of Ramon Pico's Native Cavalry but was unable to locate their hideout. Next, using good detective work, he led a posse searching the Panoche Valley in southern San Benito County (then considered part of Santa Clara County jurisdiction). But the gang countered with a network of secessionist spies and informers, and they retreated once again to Loma Prieta. Adams remained in hot pursuit and forced the gang to leave the area altogether and splinter in southern California. Sharing intelligence with his counterparts in the south, Sheriff Adams helped local Sheriff Ben Matthews track Henry to the San Bernardino Mountains. Guided by a captured gang member, Sheriff Matthews and his posse found Henry camped at San Jacinto Canyon. in a shoot-out, the awakened Henry fired his pistol three times before his body was riddled with 57 wounds. The following spring, James Mason, who had continued his criminal ways in Los Angeles County, was betrayed by an old Indian fighter he had recruited named Ben Hayfield. Hayfield was after the $500 reward posted for Mason and in the dark of night, while camped in the mountains near Fort Tejon, shot him in the neck, killing the last guerilla instantly.[17]

Sheriff John Adams walked tall, respected by other California lawmen and his grateful community. He had smashed the Ingram Partisans and rid the Central Coast region of the scourge of the Mason-Henry gang. In doing so, he had broken the back of any real threat from California secessionists and thus played his role in preserving the Union. No gold, silver, nor organized and armed military units, ever left the state to aid the Confederacy.

Notes:

1. John Boessenecker, *Badge and Buckshot. Lawlessness in Old California*, Norman: University of Oklahoma Press, 1953, pp. 3-4.

2. "Old Courthouse History," The Superior Court of California, County of Santa Clara, https://www.scscourt.org>community>och-history, retrieved Jan. 19, 2022.

3. Ibid.

4. Chris Di Salvo, *San Jose & Silicon Valley. Primed for the 21st Century*, Montgomery, Alabama: Community Communications, 1997, p. 19.

5. J. G. Kearney, *Not of the Ruling Power. Captain Ingram's Partisan Rangers in California*, Bloomington, IN: Xlibris (self-publishing), 2016.

6. Ibid.

7. Ibid.

8. "California Civil War History," American Civil War Homepage, http://www.thomaslegion.net>americancivilwar.>calif, retrieved Jan. 20, 2022.

9. "California's role in the Civil War," The Cannon's Mouth, California Historical Artillery Society, Fremont, CA, October 2016, retrieved Jan. 20, 2022.

10. John Boessenecker, *Badge and Buckshot. Lawlessness in Old California*, Norman OK: University of Oklahoma Press, 1953, pp. 136-137.

11. Phil Reader, "Copperheads, Sesech Men and Confederate Guerillas: Pro-Confederate Activities in Santa Cruz County during the Civil War," It is Not My

Intention to be Captured, Local History, Santa Cruz Public Libraries, https://historysantacruzpl.org>files>original.

12. John Boessenecker, *Badge and Buckshot*, op. cit. p. 141.

13. Ibid.

14. Ibid. pp. 149-150.

15. Edwin A. Beilharz and Donald O. DeMers Jr., *San Jose: California's First City*, Tulsa, OK: Continental Heritage Press, 1980, pp. 109-115.

16. John Boessenecker, op. cit. pp. 152-157.

17. Phil Reader, op. cit.

Chapter 7

"Pronto!"

"SIR-Pursuant to the Statute in such cases you are hereby invited to be present at the execution of Tiburcio Vasquez, at the Jail of said county, in San Jose, on the 19th day of March, A.D. 1875, at 1 ½ o'clock P.M."

–J.H. Adams, Sheriff

In the cattle-towns of the Old West, like Dodge City or Fort Worth, lawmen were often simply the meanest dog in the pack. Many were as nasty, fearless, corrupt and violent as the bad guys. Sometimes they were hard to distinguish. But as communities matured, integrity and competence came to be as important as strength and courage. Modern police work using ballistics, forensics and DNA analysis were still in the future, but efficient administrative skills and the new art of deductive reasoning were beginning to play a major role in law enforcement. Sheriff Adams may have launched his political career based on his military record, or even his short stint as his father's deputy decades earlier, but by the time he stood for re-election in 1865, he was an impressive, popular candidate. His bravery had been tested under gunfire and his dogged detective work was known up and down the state. He easily outdistanced an Independent candidate named George Jefferson by almost 700 votes while a Democrat, James Huston, trailed third. Sheriff Adams would again be elected to a third term in 1867 with a narrower win over Democrat N.R. Harris. After six years, Sheriff Adams would take a brief hiatus before returning to be elected twice more: in 1871, once again defeating Harris, and 1873, topping Independent S.W. Boring by more than 250 votes. In all, he would serve as County Sheriff for a decade, an unusually long run. [1]

Law enforcement seems to have been a family affair. In 1866, William H. Hendrick, Sheriff Adams's son-in law (married to Alice Melissa) was serving as jailer. Two Indians arrested for murder and being held for Santa Cruz County, overpowered Hendrick and after a struggle took the jailer's pistol and escaped. Hendrick grabbed another gun and chased them into the street. A block away, Hendrick fired, wounding the prisoner. But the wounded escapee returned fire and Hendrick dropped dead with a bullet through his brain. The murderer hid in construction rubble nearby, but was discovered by a throng in pursuit, who quickly blasted the cowering man into eternity. His partner was quickly captured, sent to Santa Cruz and hanged three months later. [2] According the *San Jose*

Mercury report, "Mr. Hendrick was a young man held in high esteem by a large circle of friends. He was brave and fearless-too much for his own safety" [3.] He left a widow and three of Sheriff Adams's grandchildren. A cousin and namesake, John Henry Adams, was appointed assistant jailer shortly thereafter. Adams's own son, William Humboldt, would be his deputy in the 1870's, marking the third generation of the family to hold that position.

In the years following the Civil War, many ranchers had transitioned from raising cattle and sheep to growing hay and grain. Europeans introduced varieties of grape rootstock to begin producing their accustomed wine. Jesuits opened the first college in California at the mission in Santa Clara and the first public college west of the Mississippi was founded in San Jose. The coming of the railroad signaled a real estate boom. Orchards soon dotted the Santa Clara Valley, which became the world's leading producer of canned and dried fruit. Gold was still being extracted from the Sierra foothills with new hydraulic methods and much of the silver wealth of the Nevada Comstock Lode was generating more wealth in the banks and businesses of San Francisco.

With all this progress, energy and growth came a seismic clash of cultures. The original California-born Mexicans, the *Californios,* saw their society upended and systematically discarded by the new Anglo minority. The Foreign Miner Tax laws had effectively closed any opportunity during the gold rush for *anyone* not Anglo. Discrimination, religious bigotry and anti-*Californio* racial hatred often ended in violence or heavily biased vigilante justice concluded with a lash or a noose. Even upper-class, landed *Californios* watched their influence and wealth dissipate as they struggled in the courts to save their vast land holdings. Resentment, distrust and hatred of the *gringo* festered, especially in poorer Mexican communities. In response, some *Californios* elected to return to Mexico-the original *Sal si puede!* (Get out if you can!). Most remained to face indignities and hostility. In return, many young *Californio* men resorted to living outside the Anglo law and entered a lifetime of banditry, challenging the local lawmen to catch them if they could. One of those *bandidos,* Joaquin Murrieta, became a legendary folk hero to the local population as the Mexican Robin Hood of the Gold Rush. A decade later his successor as the dashing champion of his people would be Tiburcio Vasquez, who would be relentlessly hunted by Sheriff John Adams.

Joaquin Murrieta Carrillo was born in Mexico and was lured to California with his family during the gold rush. However, by 1851, he had joined a vicious gang preying upon Anglos, Hispanics, and Chinese with equal dispassion, protected

– often out of fear – by the large Mexican population. When the gang was apprehended by militia in southern California and its leader hung, Murrieta returned to the goldfields and embarked upon a short but blood-splattered crime spree of his own. State rangers pursued Murrieta through the foothills into the central valley, eventually learning his hideout from a captured informant. Murrieta was killed in a running gun battle by Los Angeles Deputy Sheriff Harry Love in July 1853, his severed head preserved in alcohol as evidence. (The severed head was displayed in San Francisco until it was destroyed in the great earthquake and fire of 1906.) [4]

The California press had followed Murrieta's exploits with hyperbolic fascination, whipping the fearful Anglo population into a fever. Most every crime in the state became somehow attributed to Murrieta. Within a year of his death, fictionalized, highly imaginary accounts of his life began to be published, picturing Murrieta as an avenging angel to his Anglo tormentors who had allegedly raped his wife and hung his brother. Other dramatic renderings, including ballads and poems followed, each one enhancing the romantic view of this fighter against injustice. By the time venerable California scholar Herbert Bancroft endorsed the legend of the Mexican Robin Hood, it was solidified in the public consciousness. Evidence that Murrieta had been a vicious thief and killer, and that the rape, the lynching and the inflated rewards placed on his dismembered head, never happened, fell on deaf ears. The public wanted a good story.[5.] Historical facts notwithstanding, by the early twentieth century the legends surrounding Joaquin Murrieta (and Tiburcio Vasquez a decade later) had morphed into the prototype for the original heavily romanticized, but entertaining, stories of Zorro, first published in 1919 as *The Curse of Capistrano* by Johnston McCulley, a pulp fiction writer. The literary evolutionary line descends from Zorro to Batman, the caped crusader, and even dual-identity Superman. But more importantly, the story of these bandits fits into the Latin tradition of the bandit as social revolutionary and found a home in the heart of Hispanics longing for a hero resisting Anglo suppression of their culture.

Following the gold rush and statehood, Monterey was no longer the Mexican capital of Alta California. But it remained a predominantly Mexican town. Attracted by high cattle prices and *Californio* women, Monterey became a magnet for new arrivals. The *Californio* men of Monterey resented the new arrivals and were protective of their womenfolk. "Monterey quickly became one of the most violent communities in America...During the 1850s Monterey was a gunfighters' town that made Dodge City, Deadwood and Tombstone look peaceful by comparison." [5]

This was the environment Tiburcio Vasquez grew up in, one in which violence and thievery were commonplace and no one backed down from a slight or insult, much less a grievous wrong. Everyone carried a six gun or bowie knife. "[Many} *Californios* simply saw little wrong in stealing from the very Anglos who had appropriated their land and their heritage...*Californio bandidos* knew the country better than Anglo newcomers, were the best horsemen and rode the best saddle animals. With wide networks of family and friends willing to aid them, many easily eluded capture. And though Tiburcio had seen violent criminals sometimes paid for misdeeds with their lives, the lesson that the nineteen-year-old learned in Monterey was an important one: in gold rush California a man could commit murder and get away with it." [6]

By the time he had turned seventeen, Vasquez had already been involved in a murder. For the better part of the next two decades, he devoted his life to robbery, cattle rustling and horse theft, punctuated by blazing gunfire. Although he never admitted to murder, always blaming someone else, evidence proves otherwise. On three occasions, he was convicted of grand larceny and sentenced to prison at San Quentin and neither multiple failed escape efforts nor release seemed to rehabilitate him. Indeed, prison was a laboratory for learning criminal behavior and many of his fellow inmates would ride with his gang.

In some ways Vasquez defied the image of a ruthless killer. Short in stature, but athletic, he was an exceptional horseman, participating in Sunday horse races in various communities and often winning the prize money. Bilingual, he cultivated the image of an educated gentleman rather than a *vaquero* (cowboy), dressing in fashionable suits, colorful vests and polished boots. He wore a trimmed beard of medium length and carefully cut and combed his hair. He was reportedly thought handsome by the *senoritas*, and he was enormously attracted to them. He loved to enchant the *senoritas* at the various *bailes* (dances) with his grace as a dancer, his guitar playing and recitation of poetry-all aimed at seduction. His resume of sexual conquests was extensive, and he fathered several children, though he never married. At times he could exhibit fine manners and great courtesy, even to adversaries. At other times, he was coldly cruel and merciless. Wrapping himself in the *serape* of cultural champion, he could also turn against his fellow *Californios.* Many of those who protected him in the folds and valleys of central California did so out of fear as much as from admiration.

Vasquez first came to the attention of Sheriff Adams in 1864. Recently released from San Quentin prison, Vasquez had joined a gang of cattle thieves in the Monterey area. The gang rustled cattle and drove them to market in southern California, then stole more horses and cattle on the return trip north. The gang included his cousin Faustino Lorenzana, who was well known to authorities as a petty criminal in the Branciforte district of Santa Cruz County. Lorenzana had been indicted for assault with a deadly weapon, but the charges had been dropped on a technicality. On a June evening Faustino and Vasquez were gambling in a saloon in the Spanish Town miners camp at New Almaden Mines, over the hill in Santa Clara County. Spanish Town at the mines was a popular hideout for *bandidos* and the scene of much violence. A local butcher named Joseph Pelligrini had also been playing cards and the cousins followed him home. Lorenzana and Vasquez broke into his house and robbed Pelligrini, leaving the butcher stabbed and otherwise carved up on his bedroom floor. At an inquest, Sheriff Adams ironically found that the only bilingual interpreter available to help question the witnesses was Vasquez, himself. The inquest ruled Pelligrini had died at the hand of some person or persons unknown. Sheriff Adams soon learned information implicating Vasquez and Lorenzana, but it was insufficient to arrest them. Adams closely adhered to the law and protocol but made public his belief in Vasquez's guilt. By then, Vasquez had quickly relocated to Sonoma County.

Years later, Vasquez continued to deny involvement in the Pelligrini murder, claiming the unjust accusations were partially responsible for his life of crime. [7.] It would be the first of many interactions between Sheriff Adams and the elusive Vasquez.

The following year Faustino Lorenzana, along with his brother Pedro and another man, were indicted on murder charges in Santa Cruz County. Pedro Lorenzana was taken from the local jail by an angry mob which weighted him down and dumped him from the Willow Street wharf into Monterey Bay. Faustino fled to Vallecitos in the Panoche Valley of San Benito County, a favorite hideout of both Joaquin Murrieta and Tiburcio Vasquez. After a brief stealth visit to family back in the Santa Cruz area, Lorenzana tangled with Santa Cruz County Sheriff Ambrose Calderwood, stabbing him in the eye. The following year the new sheriff, Albert Jones, was ambushed by Lorenzana in the mountains above Wadell Creek, north of Santa Cruz. In August 1870, Lorenzana was herding rustled cattle from Santa Clara back to Santa Barbara. He was followed by San Jose detective O.N. Ames. Surprised while drunk under a tree near Montecito, Lorenzana exchanged gunfire with eight posse members before a taking a pistol ball in the head. His corpse displayed 16 wounds.

At one point Vasquez began adding stagecoach robbery to his repertoire. An 1871 heist of the Los Angles-bound coach north of the Salinas River yielded only an empty Wells Fargo express box. but resulted in a Wells Fargo reward for each of the bandits. Vasquez and the others rode hard into the Saucelito Valley south of Pacheco Pass in the Coast Range. Among the other outlaws were Procopio Bustamonte, nephew of Joaquin Murrieta, and Juan Soto. They were pursued by a posse co-led by Nick Harris, who had replaced Sheriff Adams in Santa Clara County for a term, and Alameda County Sheriff Henry N. Morse, a Spanish-speaking, highly regarded *pistolero* lawman. Morse was after Soto for a previous murder and caught up with him in a small adobe nestled in the folds of the Coast Range. Backed up by Sheriff Harris, Morse engaged in a furious running gun battle with Soto, who fired wildly with six-guns in either hand as he raced around the adobe for his horse to escape. Several times Morse ducked or dived to avoid being hit. After reloading, the outlaw charged Morse, who put a Spencer rifle ball into Soto's shoulder. A second round took off the top of the *bandido's* head. The protracted gunfight, witnessed by Sheriff Harris, burnished the Alameda lawman's reputation as much as the Ingram shoot-out had done for Adams's image. Sheriff Adams later discounted Soto's possible guilt and downplayed Morse's heroism. For many years Adams and Morse would engage in professional rivalry, showing a streak of jealousy in Sheriff Adams's character. [8]

As with Joaquin Murrieta, stories about Tiburcio Vasquez often took on a life of their own. One story told of Vasquez and some associates robbing a pair of sheepherders driving a wagon west of Fresno. After being relieved of some twenty dollars and their watches, one of the victims asked for the bandits to return five dollars so they could eat on their return trip. Vasquez reportedly returned half that amount. [9] A similar tale, greatly enhanced, involves Henry Miller, the Cattle King, and an encounter with Vasquez.

While driving over Pacheco Pass, the cattle baron was stopped by the bandit, Vasquez, who demanded cash and jewelry. Miller, stared at the pointed pistols and obliged, handing over $200 in twenty-dollar gold pieces, then asked for a gold piece returned for expenses on the long trip back to San Francisco. Somewhat perplexed, Vasquez handed back the coin. Two years later, as Miller lunched in a San Miguel saloon, he recognized the voice of Tiburcio Vasquez. Miller, who owned much of California (It was said one could ride from Mexico to Oregon on Miller land) was not intimidated by a mere outlaw and approached Vasquez to confirm his identity. Vasquez, again perplexed, acknowledged his identity and Miller placed a $20 gold piece on the bar, saying he always repaid his debts, before walking out of the saloon.[10.] The story, set in Santa Cruz, has also been retold substituting Sheriff Adams for Henry Miller and a similar anecdote can be found regarding the cattle king of the New Mexico Territory, John Tunstall, though with different outlaws. Whether Vasquez habitually refunded part of his loot is unlikely, and all these stories may be apocryphal, but they illustrate the desire to associate somehow with the growing legend of Tiburcio Vasquez.

In 1873, Vasquez planned his most audacious heist to date, moving up from robbing stagecoaches to trains. He set his gunsight on the pay-car of the Southern Pacific Railroad at a bridge just beyond the Twenty-One-Mile House on the Monterey Road between San Jose and Gilroy (now in the City of Morgan Hill). Before they could pull off the robbery, the railroad company was alerted. Frustrated, Vasquez decided to rob the Twenty-One-Mile House instead. The bandits tied their horses to a large oak tree in front of the white, two-story stagecoach rest stop, named for its distance from San Jose. (The giant oak, called the Vasquez Tree, still stands in front of a coffee shop. A plaque marks the spot of the bold robbery.) Covering the patrons inside with pistols and a Henry rifle, the *bandidos* made off with $800 in cash, jewelry and guns. This daring robbery happened in Sheriff Adams's backyard, and he quickly set out in pursuit, knowing he was after Vasquez. Vazquez eluded the posse, hiding out in and around the San Benito County town of Hollister. The outlaw seemed to know every move the Sheriff's posse made. With confidence he next planned to rob not a single store but an entire town. [11]

The crime became known as the Tres Pinos Tragedy. In his boldest exploit yet, Vasquez and four others-Clodovio Chavez, Teodoro Moreno, Romulo Gonzales and Abdon Leiva-rode into the small village of Tres Pinos (now Paicines) south of Hollister. For three hours they terrorized the sleepy community, robbing the store, hotel, private homes and all the inhabitants. In the process of stealing enough loot to require eight stolen pack horses, but netting only a couple thousand dollars, the *bandidos* also killed three men. Vasquez almost certainly killed a deaf man named George Redford who couldn't hear the command to lie down. As Redford ran for his life, Vasquez fired his Henry rifle, killing him instantly. Then Vasquez put a .44 caliber slug through the closed door of the hotel, into the heart of proprietor Leander Davison inside, who died in his wife's arms. As the gang made their getaway, a townsperson raced twelve miles to Hollister to raise the alarm. News of the "Tres Pinos Tragedy", as it was called in the press, quickly spread statewide. Sheriff Adams abandoned his re-election campaigning to rush to Hollister but was able to only enlist a half-dozen men for a posse, and sufficient time had elapsed for the *bandidos* to make good their escape. [12.] For the next year Tiburcio Vasquez would be the most-hunted man in California history and the most- wanted criminal in America.

After the Tres Pinos Tragedy, the Vasquez gang split up. Vasquez was rejoined by Abdon Leiva near Elizabeth Lake in Los Angeles County. Levia was accompanied by his wife Rosario. Levia, already disenchanted with gang life after the Tres Pinos murders, also suspected his wife of having an affair with Vasquez. In fact, she was pregnant with Vasquez's child. After heated words and death threats between the two outlaws, Leiva slipped away and found Sheriff Adams. Sheriff Adams had tracked Vasquez relentlessly through the heat of the San Joaquin Valley summer into the mountains above Los Angeles, on several occasions close enough for a sighting or even an exchange of gunfire. One favorite hideout was the unusual diagonal outcroppings about 40 miles north of Los Angeles, now known as Vasquez Rocks County Park. Each time Vasquez got away. Adams did encounter Romulo Gonzales but failed to recognize him and let him go without arrest. At Fort Tejon, Adams telegraphed Los Angeles County Sheriff William R. "Billy" Rowland, a popular, part-Hispanic lawman, to meet him at Lake Elizabeth. The net was closing. Meanwhile

Leiva had surrendered to Sheriff Rowland's posse. In return for leniency, or possibly immunity, Leiva made a complete confession, detailing participants and events at Twenty-One-Mile House, Tres Pinos and several other reported crime scenes. Leaving Sheriff Rowland to continue the search for Vasquez in the southland, Sheriff Adams returned to home base with captured evidence linking Vasquez to the crimes. Abdon Leiva was brought north to Monterey County jail. After his nearly 500-mile manhunt, an exhausted Sheriff Adams was gratified to find he had been re-elected for a fifth term. [13]

Tiburcio Vasquez found himself in a pincer movement, with Sheriff Rowland's posse actively combing the southern mountains and Sheriff Adams in pursuit from the north in San Benito County, out toward the New Idria Mines. As result, he was continually on the move, harbored by relatives or supportive *campesinos*. His original Tres Pinos gang had dissolved: Teodoro Moreno had been captured and sentenced to San Quentin prison, Romulo Gonzales had fled to Mexico, and Abdon Leiva was in custody. Only Clodovio Chavez remained with the leader. With some new recruits the gang committed a series of robberies and stagecoach hold-ups. Their activities climaxed the day after Christmas with a audacious daylight raid on the town of Kingston in Fresno County, plundering the homes and establishments for more than $2,500,

174

although no one in Kingston was injured. Having abandoned his lover, Rosario Leiva, after she miscarried and fell into depression, the not-so-gallant Vasquez felt free to roam at will from the Coast Range in central California to the surrounds of Los Angeles.[14]

With Vasquez sightings on every hilltop, Mexicans and *Californios* were increasingly under suspicion and less inclined to aid the wanted bandido. Many wealthy or upper-class *Californios* now sided against the bandit. Governor Newton Booth approved a legislative act appropriating some $15,000 to underwrite a massive dragnet to finally bring the Vasquez gang to justice. A reward ultimately offered $8,000 for his capture or $6,000 for his corpse. Governor Booth tapped Alameda County Sheriff Morse to lead the first state-wide manhunt since the efforts to track down Joaquin Murrieta more than twenty years before. Sheriff Adams was keenly disappointed at this selection of his professional rival Morse to lead the posse, rather than himself. Also selected to join the posse was former Santa Cruz County Sheriff Ambrose Calderwood, who had been partially blinded in the knife attack by Vasquez's cousin, Faustino Lorenzana. The manhunt would become the longest of the century-two months of hard riding over some 2,700 miles of California landscape. [14]

Ultimately, it was not his brazen daylight robberies or the bloody trail he left across the state that led to Vasquez's undoing. Rather it was his lust for the ladies, including his own niece. His scorned and conflicted former lover, Rosario Leiva, hoping to reconcile with her incarcerated husband, had given evidence under subpoena to Sheriff Adams, pointing the finger at the Vasquez gang for several crimes. After scouring his known hideouts between Monterey and the Tehachapi Mountains for over a month, Sheriff Morse correctly guessed Vasquez had retreated to southern California once again. A *San Francisco Chronicle* newspaperman named A.B. Henderson, riding with the Morse posse, serialized the manhunt for hungry readers, inadvertently apprising Vasquez of the posse's progress. By spring Vasquez was hiding out at an adobe tavern, near what is now West Hollywood, run by "Greek George" Caralambo. The real attraction was his latest flame, Caralambo's sister-in-law Modesta Lopez.[15]

Vasquez continued to rob with seeming impunity in the southland. Citizens of Los Angeles grew increasingly nervous about a possible raid on their town. In fact, Vasquez was seriously considering robbing a Los Angeles bank, one of very few yet in the state. Los Angeles Sheriff Rowland seemed reluctant to aggressively hunt Vasquez, for fear of alienating his Hispanic constituency, and he began to suffer criticism, including publicly in the *Chronicle* for his inactivity. Sheriff Morse received a tip that Vasquez stayed at Greek George's home. The informant may have been the *novio* (boyfriend) of Vasquez's niece, defending her honor after she gave birth to Vasquez's illegitimate child, or possibly his jealous current lover. In any event Morse approached Greek George and offered a slice of the large reward. Sheriff Rowland was forced to act and delegated his undersheriff, Albert Johnson to take a posse to Greek George's. The posse included Los Angeles police detective Emil Harris, Chief of Police Frank Hartley and newspaperman George Beers, who would become part of the story as well as an early Vasquez biographer.

After surreptitiously leaving town to avoid detection by one of Vasquez's many informers, the posse rode into the dark, capturing several gang members enroute to Greek George's. The posse arrived unnoticed by lying prone in a wagon bed "like sardines". They quietly surrounded the adobe building. Emil Harris burst through the door and confronted Vasquez who tried to escape out a window. Harris fired his Henry rifle, wounding the outlaw superficially in the side. Outside, other deputies fired at the man bolting for his horse. Chief Hartley unloaded both barrels of his shotgun and buckshot crashed into its target's head and arm. Critically injured and loosing blood from eight wounds, the man was identified as Tiburcio Vasquez. On May 14, 1874, law officers finally had their man.

Once incarcerated in the Los Angeles County jail, Vasquez received proper medical attention and his many wounds began to heal. Because no rail line yet existed between Los Angeles and northern California, the prisoner was extradited north onboard the coastal steamer *Senator*. Unable to dock at Monterey in rough seas, the ship sailed on through the Golden Gate to San Francisco, where Sheriff John Adams and his Monterey counterpart, Sheriff J.B. Smith, awaited. As Sheriff Adams recorded in his pocket diary and expense book, "Tiburcio Vasquez arrived in San Francisco in custody of Sheriff Rowland and Undersheriff Johnson and Deputy Mitchel. Visited him in prison. Remained in City. Paid for goods $6.00." [16]

Sheriff Adams was no doubt relieved to see his foe safely in custody, but probably secretly regretted not having been the one to bring him in himself. After a brief stay in the San Francisco jail, and a photography session (Vasquez would get a cut of the sales of his *carte-de-visite* which the public scooped up at 25 cents each) Vasquez was escorted by Sheriff Adams on the train to the Monterey County jail in Salinas. When court opened in Hollister, county seat for San Benito-site of the Tres Pinos murders-public sentiment ran so strongly against

Vasquez that District Judge David Belden granted a change of venue to Santa Clara County and its secure jail. The *bandido* found himself in final custody of his nemesis John Hicks Adams. [17]

Carefully guarded in Sheriff Adams's stout jail, Vasquez recovered fully from his wounds and enjoyed the life of a celebrity. He entertained a steady stream of visitors, eventually numbering over a thousand a day. On July 21, 1874, Sheriff Adams noted in his diary, "Busy at jail attending to visitors wishing to see Vasquez." [18.] Among those visitors were former robbery victims, infatuated young ladies -both Anglo and Hispanic-, respectful *Californios* and the simply curious. Vasquez freely signed autographs and his jail cell was filled with floral bouquets. In several conversations with Sheriff Adams and correspondent George Beers, Vasquez equivocated on details of his past but steadfastly denied ever killing anyone. While freely admitting with regret having led a life of crime, he maintained it was caused by personal slights and general repression and injustice at the hands of the Anglo Invaders who had arrived in California. He claimed his dream was the organization of an armed rebellion that would return [southern] California to Mexican rule. In truth, members of his own gang did not often follow him for long. As for engendering loyalty, Vasquez had been ultimately betrayed by men-and women-

179

from his inner circle. At one point Vasquez was confronted by his former henchman turned betrayer Abdon Leiva. The cuckold and the bandit shook hands but engaged in no conversation.[19]

After issuance of several continuances due to difficulty in locating witnesses, trial was scheduled for January 5, 1875, in the 20th District Court, Judge Belden presiding. The prosecution team was led by State Attorney General John Lord Love. Vasquez was represented by attorneys P.B. Tully, W.H. Collins and J.A. Moultrie. Witnesses included Abdon Leiva and his estranged wife Rosario and several citizens of Tres Pinos who had witnessed the shootings there. Sheriff Adams took the stand, showing recovered evidence from the robbery that corroborated Leiva's testimony. The trial lasted four days before a packed gallery in the second-floor courtroom. In a lengthy closing argument, defense counsel Collins appealed to the emotions of the jury, blaming society for Vasquez's deeds. Prosecutor Love rebutted with facts and called for conviction of murder in the first degree. The case went to the jury on the afternoon of January 9th. At eight o'clock that evening the jury returned its verdict: "We, the jury, find the defendant guilty of murder in the First Degree, and affix the Death Penalty." A motion for retrial was denied and Vasquez was remanded to Sheriff Adams for execution by hanging scheduled for March

19. [20] An appeal was soon rejected by the State Supreme Court and Governor Romulado Pacheco, himself a *Californio,* denied a reprieve.

Awaiting his destiny, Vasquez became reflective. He wrote poetry and bemoaned his lifelong obsession with women as his ultimate downfall. Family members paid him a visit. In conversation with Sheriff Adams, he demonstrated remorse and reflected on the pain he had caused his family. He wrote final messages asking his family for forgiveness and another advising his former associates to not try to avenge his death. On the evening before his scheduled execution, one of his last conversations was with young Willie Adams, the Sheriff's jailer-son, who brought him a final cigar. To the end, he never admitted being a killer. [21]

Executions had been rare in Santa Clara County and Sheriff Adams had to borrow a gallows from Sacramento County. Executions were a public event. Trains disgorged hundreds of passengers who swelled the hotels, all anxious to catch a glimpse of the spectacle. Per custom, Sheriff Adams distributed 300 printed invitations to dignitaries, fellow law enforcement officers and the press. Among those accepting the invitation were James B. Hume, who had worked with Adams after the Bullion Bend Robbery and was now a special agent for Wells Fargo & Co., Alameda County Sheriff Henry Morse and even legendary Deadwood *pistolero* lawman Seth Bullock, who was in California on official business. The walled courtyard was jammed with observers and hundreds more climbed nearby balconies, roofs and trees to peer into the jail yard.

At the appointed hour, Vasquez was escorted outside and mounted the gallows, accompanied by a large contingent of law officers, many of whom had spent long days in the saddle hunting this quarry. A priest offered a prayer. Vasquez stoically accepted the bindings, noose and hood. At a signal from Sheriff John Hicks Adams, the trap doors opened and California's most infamous *bandido* fell quickly to his death. He was officially pronounced dead within a quarter hour. He was yet only 39 years old. His final word had been the Spanish for "Quick": *Pronto!*

Among the many stories that surrounded Vasquez was the notion that he and Sheriff Adams had actually been friends. One tale goes that once while Adams was away chasing Vasquez, the wily bandit boldly doubled back to the Adams homestead and partook of a meal with Mrs. Adams. This is highly unlikely; their acquaintance would have been one of wary respect rather than friendship and there is no historical evidence supporting the story. And the most enduring myth about the bandit was his role as a 19th century Robin Hood, robbing rich Anglos and sharing the wealth with downtrodden *Californios.* In fact, the victims of his banditry were often neither rich nor exclusively Anglo. If Vasquez generously reimbursed the hospitality of his protectors, well, it's easy to be free with someone else's money. Like Joaquin Murrieta before him, Vasquez cultivated this myth of popular hero to protect himself – and probably to impress the *senoritas.*

After a wake at his cousin's home in Santa Clara, followed by a Catholic mass in Mission Santa Clara, Vasquez was buried in the old mission cemetery. In a strange interpretation of history, he became to many a symbol of their own struggle for social justice. To this day, fresh flowers appear on the *bandido's* grave. In his diary entry for March 19, 1875, Sheriff Adams wrote: "Tiburcio Vasquez hung at 1:38 min. PM. Died without a struggle. Very busy and exciting day for one – great crowd in attendance. Everything went off [as planned]."[22]

Notes:

1. *Pen Pictures from the Garden of the World-or-Santa Clara County*, H.S. Foote ed. Chicago: Lewis Publishing Co., 1888, pp. 112-115.

2. Eugene Sawyer, *History of Santa Clara County California*, Historic Record Co., 1922.

3. "Terrible Tragedy," *San Jose Mercury*, February 15, 1866.

4. William Mero, Joaquin Murrieta: "Literary Fiction or Historical Fact?," https://www.cocohistory.org>essays-murrieta, retrieved Jan. 25, 2022.

5. John Bossenecker, *Bandido. The life and Times of Tiburcio Vasquez*, Norman: University of Oklahoma Press, 2010, p. 36.

6. Ibid. pp.52-53.

7. Phil Reader, "Charole: The Life of Branciforte Bandido Faustino Lorenzana," Local History-Santa Cruz Public Libraries, https://history.antacruzpl.org/omeka, retrieved Jan. 5, 2022.

8. Boessenecker, op. cit. pp. 137-139.

9. Ibid. p. 208.

10. Museum exhibit, Gilroy Historical Museum, Gilroy, CA.

11. Bosesenecker, op. cit. pp. 210-212.

12. Sawyer, op. cit.

13. Ibid.

14. Boessenecker. op. cit., pp. 277-327.

15. Ibid. pp. 289-308.

16. John Hicks Adams, Diary entry, May 27, 1874.

17. Clyde Arbuckle, *History of San Jose, San Jose: Memorabilia of San Jose* (pub.), 1986 pp. 339-340.

18. John Hicks Adams, Diary entry, July 21, 1874.

19. Clyde Arbuckle, op. cit.

20. Ibid.

21. Boessenecker, op. cit. pp. 349-358.

22. John Hicks Adams, Diary entry, March 19, 1875.

Chapter 8

One Gang Too Many

"If I am to protect the people, I must have funds to do it."

–U.S. Marshal Crawley P. Duke, 1878

In the days following the execution of Tiburcio Vasquez, the prominence of Sheriff Adams as a California lawman was possibly matched only by his rival across the bay, Henry Morse. To the south Sheriff William Rowland was busy rehabilitating his reputation after dragging his feet in the pursuit of Vasquez. In San Jose, inmates of the county jail had an unusual complaint. The ghost of Vasquez was reported to have appeared in the jail, "snorting and cavorting around in the most ridiculous manner. Vasquez had said he would come back after he had explored the regions of the lower country" [1]

While the rare public executions drew enormous public attention, the routine police work of a county sheriff continued. The docket was always full of cases involving arson, horse thievery, public drunk and disorderliness, burglaries, grand larceny, assaults and occasionally murders. Sheriffs spent

187

much effort aiding each other catching and jailing fugitives from other jurisdictions, accompanying prisoners to and from jails or the state penitentiary, and even delivering the criminally insane to the state facility at Stockton - "Went to Stockton and back with insane person. Expenses $13.50." Appearing at countless court hearings or trials, and the never-ending paperwork took time away for forming a posse and going after outlaws with arrest warrants and six-guns.

Sheriff Adams kept a pocket diary in which he cryptically recorded his activities but carefully kept track of his expenses. Many of the entries are pedestrian: "Busy all Day;" "District Court Appearances." Some entries even mentioned the weather: "Cool and Foggy" or "Pleasant." He also demonstrated paying attention to his family: "Visited children; Nellie Quite Sick;" or "Wife Better." But other entries offer more insight into his job and even foreshadow his future, such as "Went to San Francisco after counterfeiters. Had a talk with _____ Bennett about mines at Eureka [Nevada]."[2]

A month after the excitement of the Vasquez execution, a reflective Sheriff Adams decided not to run for renomination for Sheriff. As reported in the *San Jose Daily Mercury:* "He says he has had the office several terms and is now willing to retire in favor of others. This is to be very much regretted, for as an officer Sheriff Adams is without a peer. Experienced in

188

office, a shrewd detective and a brave man, his name has become a terror to evil-doers, and it will be hard to fill his place. His loss will be great, not only to Santa Clara County, but also to the state. With such men as Chavez (the last of the Tres Pinos Murders gang) and Gonzales at large Capt. Adams can illy be spared from his office and we hope he may yet be induced to consent to serve the people another term." [3]

Whether that editorial endorsement was persuasive to the sheriff is unknown. Perhaps Adams was unable to leave the stage with the lights shining so brightly. Possibly he knew he had more to contribute, or simply wasn't ready to retire. For whatever reason, he changed his mind, and that September ran for office as a Republican once again, seeking a sixth term. For the first time in his political career, the coattails of Lincoln's Grand Old Party and his own reputation were not sufficient to carry the day. He lost to Nicholas R. Harris by vote count of 2,854 to 2,140 in an election that saw Democrats sweep to victory in most local offices. Harris had previously served as county sheriff from 1870-1872, when Adams had decided not to run. This time the voters had chosen for Adams to retire.

In March 1876, Sheriff Adams handed over the keys to the county jail and his badge to incoming Sheriff Harris. After years of stressful dedication to the job, Adams was free to explore other options and even take a vacation. As comfortable

189

outdoors as inside a building, Adams had not enjoyed a break since taking a ten-day rejuvenation trip to Mt. Whitney in 1873, where he had scaled the nation's highest peak and planted the stars and stripes on its summit, describing the view as indescribable grandeur and beauty.[4] For many, retirement holds the promise of golden years, but unfulfilled time can turn leaden and as disappointing as iron pyrite- fool's gold. Captain Adams turned his attention back to his former occupation: mining.

The former 49er had never lost his interest in mining. As early as 1869, he had been a trustee of the John Dare Silver Mining Company. Located in the Silver Mountains in northwest Nevada, the Dare mines were among scores of mines established on either side of the Humboldt Range in the years immediately after the Civil War. Before the completion of the transcontinental railroad, such flourishing towns as Star City or Unionville (home to Mark Twain for a while) had to be supplied by wagon from Marysville in California. The mines produced both gold and silver ores.[5]

While the Quicksilver Mine at New Almaden had become a bonanza, especially after the discovery of gold drove the demand for mercury to record levels, there were other cinnabar deposits in the south Santa Clara Valley to be found. In the early 1860s cinnabar was discovered on the John Piercy property a dozen miles southeast of San Jose. The North Almaden Quicksilver Mining Company operated a small, under-capitalized enterprise there before becoming discouraged and folding. Years later an experienced prospector named Charles Hanson examined the abandoned mine sites and found evidence of a major strike. The South Almaden Mining Company was formed with Hanson as superintendent and Captain J. H. Adams as president. By 1876, the mine was operating, producing more ore than it had furnace capability. With further prospecting, Captain Adams discovered a rich deposit of metal. In order to turn their discoveries into profits, the company officers planned to issue stock to fund their infrastructure development and purchase of newer, larger furnaces. [6]

In Fall, 1876, at the invitation of Captain Adams, a reporter for the *San Jose Weekly Mercury* inspected the South Almaden quicksilver mines. He wrote, "There are the very best grounds for belief that the South Almaden Quicksilver mines will soon command attention in the marts of trade, bearing close resemblance to that which the New Almaden has so long enjoyed a monopoly of in this country...Rock, carrying cinnabar very strong, is now being taken out near the surface on both sides of Silver Creek {as well as in} the ledges cropping out in several distinct places on the brow of the hill to the west." [7]

By the following spring, the mine had been operating for a year but work there had slowed. During the first four months of 1877, the mine produced one hundred flasks of mercury. Although there was an abundance of ore available, the company found it more expensive to process the ore than the value of the mercury extracted, given a decline in market price. The company was busy digging a 200-foot-deep shaft, expecting to find higher grade ore deposits. The company was described as an exclusively Santa Clara County enterprise built up by home industry, energy and capital of local investors. [8] Though outwardly optimistic, the mine owners were finding their operation unprofitable and increasingly expensive to continue. By summer, Captain Adams was once again considering seeking the Republican nomination for another term as sheriff. *The Pioneer* newspaper reported that Capt. J.H. Adams has concluded that the shrievalty (sheriff's job) is worth going for and so he will be a candidate." [9] Captain Adams, himself, published the following announcement in the *San Jose Weekly Mercury:*

> *"Within the past few weeks, a large number of influential Republicans of the city of San Jose, and in other parts of the county, have, by personal*

solicitation and by letters, most earnestly pressed me to consent to become a candidate for the nomination of Sheriff before our next Republican Convention...I had not intended to again appear as a candidate for office, but as the desire has been so generally and sincerely expressed that I present myself as a candidate before the convention, I beg you to allow me to say, after due reflection, that I deem it my duty to do so. If in my judgment I can be of service to the party ass a nominee, I have to say that my past record will indicate my future line of conduct.

Most, respectfully,
J.H. Adams
San Jose, June 13th, 1877" [10]

Despite several endorsements and his willingness to return to the public sphere, Captain Adams did not secure the Republican nomination. Losing the previous election had no doubt injured his pride; failing to even be nominated by his own party this time added insult to injury. The long-time sheriff's political career had come to an end. His career as a lawman had not.

Out of the public eye, Captain Adams doubled down on his mining interests. Like a compulsive gambler who feels the next card dealt will win the pot, a miner believes he will strike it rich at the next diggings, just around the next mountain.

Captain Adams turned his attention away from the diminishing productivity of the South Almaden venture toward the reports of a new bonanza to be found in the hard, sunbaked terrain of southwest Arizona.

Mining had been practiced in the southwest since the time of the Spanish conquistadors. Following the American Civil War, contingents of federal troops remained in the newly formed Territory of Arizona to safeguard against Apache raiding parties. The local economy was dependent upon the military for hard currency in addition to protection. Stagecoach lines developed, linking Fort Yuma to El Paso and Tucson into Mexico, but the cost of transportation made mining a risky venture. Only the precious metals-gold and silver-justified the effort. An old Mexican proverb warned: "in order to work a copper mine, it is first necessary to own a silver mine." During this post-Civil War period, miners began to fan out from Tucson into the mineralized region called the Patagonia District. Many of the mines were owned by syndicates far from the diggings. Pockets, and even caves, full of mineral deposits were discovered and small mines began to pockmark the landscape, the value of the lead, copper or silver ore varied greatly and without the railroad, there was no efficient way to transport the deposits. In 1874, the discovery of placer gold near Salero started a minor gold rush, bringing hundreds of hopeful Mexicans and Americans into the area.[11]

As the calendar turned to the new year of 1878, Captain Adams was deeply involved in Arizona mining ventures at the Washington Mine in the Patagonia District as well as another mine called the Lone Star. He likely had also invested in these enterprises. The next step required going to Arizona. In his 57th year, he still possessed enormous energy for the undertaking. His children were grown and married or nearly so. Their youngest son, Abraham Lincoln Adams, was already into his teenage years (his name reflecting the custom of honoring someone deeply admired-in this case the martyred Emancipator). In a decision that would prove prophetic, Adams deemed Arizona too dangerous for his wife or any of the children; once again Matilda would stay behind, surrounded by her family, waiting to hear of her husband finding his fortune. The Adams family had moved from their North 4th Street home near the courthouse and jail. The 1878 San Jose City Directory lists the family living near the corner of Ashworth Road and McLaughlin Avenue, east of Coyote Creek, in San Jose. It lists his occupation as "miner."

Sometime in January 1878, Captain Adams bought a train ticket and rode the rails to the end of the line in Arizona, then continued by stagecoach to Tucson. Established in 1775

195

as a Spanish *presidio,* Tucson was situated in a lush valley in the middle of the Sonoran Desert, It had been acquired as part of the Gadsden Purchase of 1854, which added much of southern Arizona and southwest New Mexico to the United States. The "Old Pueblo", 60 miles north of the Mexican border, was Arizona Territory's largest city and had served as the territorial capital until 1877, the year it was incorporated as a city. For the miners of Patagonia, Tucson was civilization.

Captain Adams didn't travel alone. Accompanying him were a pair of San Jose associates, Cornelius Finley and Finley's brother-in-law John Sevenoaks. (As sheriff, Adams had previously had a run-in with Sevenoaks, who had interfered with the arrest of an arson suspect in Gilroy.) Cornelius Finley was born in Delaware County, New York in 1828. He descended, coincidentally, from a formidable English mining family. Finley arrived in California in 1852, drawn by the pull of the gold rush. After mining in California, he tried his luck in the Washoe, Nevada Comstock strike. While there he became trustee of a pair of mining companies, Finley Gold and Silver Mining Co. and Haven Gold and Silver Mining Co. He served for a time as tax collector for Virginia City, Nevada, but by 1868 he had re-established himself as a furniture manufacturer in Gilroy, California. In 1871, Finley had been elected County Clerk of Santa Clara County, and he served two terms. While working in county government, Finley became associated with J.H. Adams and the two became good friends. They were both members of the Pioneer Society of Santa Clara County. It was Finley's signature that certified the execution of Tiburcio Vasquez. The forty-nine year-old Finley left his wife Amelia and three daughters in San Jose. With mining backgrounds and public service in common, Adams and Finley formed a prospecting team and headed for Arizona territory.[12]

From the terse entries in his pocket diary and account book for 1878, we know that Captain Adams and his associates looked for gold along the Russian River and Cooper Creek tributary of southern Arizona. According to Adams, *"Some prospectors [did] not [do] as good as we did. The life of a prospector is a hard one since full of _ and uncertainties."* [13] Being away from home weighed on his mind that spring. In March, he wrote *"Exceedingly glad to get a letter from home—was late news March 5th but [nevertheless] it seemed like a token of love from home and done me lots of good."* [14]

Arizona Territory in the 1870s was a world of cactus, barren desert, and rugged mountain terrain, virtually unpopulated by settlers. The native Chiricahua Apaches had been largely suppressed by federal troops stationed along the frontier. The border with Mexico was ill-defined and mostly ignored. There was no law enforcement on either side. This natural state of anarchy became a safe haven for desperadoes of all sorts. Societal miscreants fleeing the wrath of Texas Rangers or veterans of the bloody Lincoln County wars in New Mexico found sanctuary in Arizona and brought their criminal activities with them. Soon Arizona suffered an epidemic of stagecoach robberies and highwaymen holdups as the outlaws operated with impunity and their numbers grew. Almost organically, many of these new arrivals coalesced into a loosely knit, leaderless gaggle of part-time cattle rustlers and horse thieves. Operating on both sides of the border, these outlaws would steal Mexican cattle and drive the herds into Arizona and, altering the brands, trade them with local ranchers or sell them to local butchers and settlers hungry for beef. Stealing valuable horses was another profitable enterprise. Mexican authorities complained bitterly about these *gringo* incursions into Sonora and American officials countered with claims the Mexicans harbored the bandits. No one seemed to be able to do anything to curb them.

These outlaws came to be known as the Cow-Boys, a take on the long held term "c*owboy*" for cattle drover, itself derived from the Spanish word *vaquero* - one who herds *vacas* (cows). The Cow-Boys eventually numbered between one and two hundred men, the largest gang of the Old West. "This loosely organized gang would murder at least thirty-five men, steal thousands of horses and cattle, terrorize the ranchers and settlers of Southern Arizona and northern Mexico, and cause a series of international incidents. No one could stop them." [15]

Whatever law enforcement existed fell to the Territorial U.S. Marshal. In June 1878, the position belonged to Crawley P. Dake, who was under tremendous political pressure from Territorial Governor John C. Fremont – The Pathfinder, himself, now in the twilight of his career - to somehow address the series of violent holdups and livestock theft. Among the loudest voices clamoring for action were the freight and stagecoach operators who provided the territory with its links to the outside and upon which the young economy depended. Born in Ontario, Canada, Dake had grown up in New York and was a wounded Union Army veteran, having raised the 5th Michigan Cavalry unit during the Civil War, seeing action at Gettysburg. Before accepting the Arizona marshalcy, he had been deputy marshal in Detroit and had run unsuccessfully for Congress. At the time, the Department of Justice required a marshal to request funds for the pursuit and capture of each robbery suspect on an individual basis. The slow bureaucratic procedure continually frustrated Dake, who soon took to ignoring procedure and began deputizing civilians despite the restrictions under the *Posse Comitatus Act of 1878* and pursuing bandits-even into Mexico-without waiting for warrants or money. [16]

Marshal Dake's tactics began to meet with some success and by summer 1878, local authorities and even the Mexican government were cooperating with him in curtailing the *banditti,* as they were called. When Marshal Dake became aware of the presence of a renowned former California sheriff in the territory, he was encouraged by Judge Charles Silent to eagerly press Captain Adams to become deputized. For his part, Captain Adams may have felt law enforcement was part of his past and he now wanted to concentrate on his mining interests, where Cornelius Finley was superintendent of the Washington Mine and Adams was mine manager. Nevertheless, Captain Adams agreed to the role and both he and Cornelius Finley were duly sworn-in as Deputy United States Marshals on August. 23, 1878.

Managing the mine required periodic trips to Tucson for supplies, deposits and other mine business. On September 2, 1878, Adams and Finley hitched their wagon to a fresh team of horses and set off on the seventy-five-mile trip from Harshaw District to Tucson. As they had often done, they broke the trip to enjoy the hospitality of the Empire Ranch, run by partners Walter Vail, Herbert Hislop and John Harvey. According to Edward Vail, "As they arrived too late for dinner and were anxious to reach Tucson, my brother told the cook to get them a light lunch and let them go. They had a buggy and a good team of horses- I think it was a Tucson livery team of horses – so expected to make the trip quickly." [17]

Not many miles north of Empire Ranch, a Mexican bandit gang rode down from the northern Santa Rita Mountains to let their horses drink from Cienega Creek in the east fork of Davidson Canyon. The gang leader was a former Mexican revolutionary named Guadalupe Celaya who had turned to a life of banditry. His followers included Joaquin Franco, Pascual Ladrillo, Gregorio Arce, Antonio Rodriguez, possibly Gorgonio Garcia and a *mestizo* named Florentino Sais. They had been furiously evading a posse and cavalry detachment chasing them into Mexico and back for several days after robbing a couple of stagecoaches of their Wells Fargo strongboxes, the passengers' valuables and the teams of horses. Celaya had heard that a wagon carrying a mine payroll or gold dust would be traveling along the Tucson trail. He ordered his men into cover behind the boulders abutting the road and they waited.

Captain Adams and Cornelius Finley were no doubt anxious to reach Tucson before dark as they encouraged their team ahead on the rutted track, the dust settled after a recent rain. At the rattling sound of their approach the bandidos took aim and opened fire. At the retort of the rifles, the horses bolted, and Finley and Adams instinctively rose to jump from their wagon. A bullet tore into Finley's heart from behind, killing him instantly. As he fell, his boot caught in the spokes of the wagon wheel, and he bled out suspended head down on the side of the wagon. Captain Adams slapped leather as he leapt from the wagon and searched for a target to return fire. A bullet from a concealed ambusher pierced the lawman's torso, wounding him gravely if not mortally. The *bandidos* rushed to the wagon to get the anticipated strongbox. Finding none they shouted curses in Spanish. From the ground, Captain Adams mustered his ebbing strength to unleash his Colt one last time. Hearing the wounded man stir, the frustrated *bandidos* pounced on Adams and clubbed him to death with rocks. They relieved the victims of their wallets, pocket watches and weapons, including Captain Adams's ivory handled pistol, then unhitched the team from the wagon and made ready to escape. It is not known whether the *bandidos* knew that they had killed deputy U.S. marshals. Badges for the marshals did not become standard issue until the twentieth century. It likely would have made no difference to the assailants but the death of the lawmen caught the attention of the entire country.

"The murders of the two prominent Californians hit the telegraph wires and made newspapers nationwide, reinforcing

Arizona's reputation as a forbidding region peopled by wild Indians and dangerous outlaws." [18]

The Celaya gang spurred their horses south toward Mexico to make good their get-away. At or near the Empire Ranch they likely encountered some of the ranch hands and in broken English told them they had just found the corpses of two men who had been ambushed on the trail and had reported the deaths to another pair of miners. Then the gang hastily rode off. Rancher Walter Vail. feared it might have been his recent guests, Adams and Finley. Vail sent men to investigate, who confirmed the identity of the slain men and quickly buried them in shallow graves. Vail next deduced that the real killers had been the Celaya gang, themselves, and chased after the gang until a heavy rain washed out the trail. Next, he and partner John Harvey organized a posse of fifteen men to pursue them into the Mexican state of Sonora if necessary. Among the Empire Ranch cowboys were two brothers who had recently arrived in Arizona to pursue ranching, Tom and Frank McLaury. It's likely they were caught up in the pursuit of the assassins. Unknown to the McLaurys, they were distant cousins of the slain Cornelius Finley, sharing a maternal great grandfather. (Frank's given birth name was Robert and both he and his mother shared the same middle name, Findley, a family spelling variation).

According to the *Arizona Weekly Star* of September 26, Mexican *federales* had apprehended three suspected members of the Celaya gang inside Mexico, in possession of a gold watch and satchel belonging to Captain Adams. A week later two more suspects, identified as Arce and Sais, were arrested in northern Sonora and jailed at Magdalena. A pistol later identified as that belonging to Cornelius Finley (possibly on loan) was also recovered. "[19] The *Arizona Weekly Miner* reported that while in jail, the two bandits confessed to the killings and were ordered shot. [20.] Gang leader Guadalupe Celaya remained at large.

Meanwhile, armed with Winchesters and extradition papers signed by Chief Justice C.G.W. French, the Vail-Harvey posse had arrived at Magdalena to collect the prisoners but the prefect in charge would not release them without approval of the governor. Vail and Harvey rode another 150 miles to Ures, Sonora to petition Governor Vicente Mariscal to had hand over the bandits for trial in the United States. The governor professed cooperation with the Americans but said he would need authority from Mexican President Porfirio Diaz in Mexico City. The request was duly forwarded to the capital, followed by several demands from American diplomats, most falling into the black hole of international bureaucracy. The Harvey-Vail posse returned to Arizona after a month of frustration

204

without their suspected killers. Meanwhile, the Celaya gang members remained in the Sonoran jails, where they were well-treated rather than executed, and even boasted of having killed the *gringos* in Davidson Canyon. [21, 22]

News of the brutal demise of Adams and Finley filtered back to San Jose from sources in Arizona. Accounts of the murders varied slightly in detail. One reported that the bandits knew their victims and after a conversation killed them with their own guns. But the substance of the events was consistent. Finley's brother-in-law, John Sevenoaks, reported that the bodies were unearthed and sent to Tucson in zinc-lined caskets, where the entire population turned out for their funeral services before they were laid to rest in Tucson cemetery. [23.] The *San Jose Weekly Mercury* reported, "The mournful intelligence was soon spread about, and a gloom was cast over the whole community for the murdered men, besides being representative citizens of this county, had endeared themselves to all who had the pleasure of their acquaintance or friendship by their many manly qualities and the perseverance and bravery that they had so often shown under circumstances that try men's souls. They were men of character, of integrity and push, and such as a community can ill afford to lose." [24]. Captain Adams's widow, Matilda, reportedly spiraled into depression and ill-health at receiving the news.

In a solicitous letter to Captain Adams's son William, Sonoran Governor Mariscal noted that the assassins were incarcerated rather than executed. He wrote, "I have written to the City of Mexico, sending all the particulars of the deed, and I trust when Government in Washington reclaim officially of my country the extradition of those individuals, and when I shall be ordered, I will take special care to deliver them up." [25]

The remains of Adams and Finley did not remain in Tucson long. A man named Freeman B. Smith traveled from San Jose to Arizona to handle their affairs. Their caskets were exhumed and sent by rail to San Jose, where a large crowd waited at the railroad station. The bodies were laid in state at the Odd Fellows Hall, then removed to City Market Hall for religious services and lengthy oratory. The local press covered the ensuing funerals at Oak Hills Memorial Cemetery in great detail. The *San Jose Weekly Mercury* noted, "There were about a thousand persons in the procession, and at every cross street it was joined by long lines of carriages" [24.] And the *Pioneer* added, "The Beterans [sic – veterans] of the Mexican War and also the Pioneers turned out almost to a man and the other societies from every part of the county were represented in large number of their members. Besides the Military, Champions of the Red Cross and Druids, in full regalia, as well as the [listed] lodges of I.O.O.F." [26]

A hymn and a prayer concluded the solemn ceremony. Next the crowd moved to the burial site for Cornelius Finley, where the services were repeated. The graves were filled. A unit of Zouaves recognized the military service of Captain Adams with three volleys of musket fire. The crowd departed. [27] After a heroic life and martyr's death the life of John Hicks Adams had ended; however, since history is a tapestry of interwoven people and events, connections and coincidences, there is still more of his story to be told.

Notes:

1. *San Jose Daily Mercury,* April 23, 1875, p. 3.

2. John Hicks Adams, Diary entry , December 18, 1874.

3. *San Jose Daily Mercury* , April 22, 1875.

4. *San Jose Weekly Mercury,* Aug. 14, 1873.

5. Frederick Leslie Ransome, "Notes on Some Mining Districts in Humboldt County Nevada," Washington D.C.: Department of the Interior, *U.S. Geological Survey Bulletin 414,* 1909.

6. "South Almaden Quicksilver Mines," *San Jose Weekly Mercury,* June 1, 1876.

7. "South Almaden," *San Jose Weekly Mercury,* Nov. 2, 1876.

8. "South Almaden Mine," *San Jose Weekly Mercury,* May 10, 1877.

9. *The Pioneer,* June 16, 1877.

10. Card from Capt. Adams, *San Jose Weekly Mercury,* June 21, 1877.

11. Robert Lenon, "The Patagonia Area Mining Districts, Santa Cruz County Arizona 1539-1930," Chapter 3, 1998. https://www.miningfoundationssw.org, retrieved Feb. 2, 2022.

12. Pamela Potter, "A well-known lawman from California and a relative of the McLaurys were shot down in Arizona Territory," *Wild West,* August 2003, pp. 14-16, 70.

13. John Hicks Adams, pocket diary, July 24, 1878.

14. Ibid. March 19, 1878.

15. John Boessenecker, *Ride the Devil's Herd. Wyatt Earp's Epic Battle Against the West's Biggest Outlaw Gang*, Toronto: Hanover Square Press 2021, p. 36.

16. Larry D. Ball, *The United States Marshals of New Mexico and Arizona Territories 1846-1912*, Albuquerque: University of New Mexico Press, 1940, pp. 107-113.

17. "Vail, Hislop and Harvey 1877-1878," Empire Ranch Foundation, p. 2, https://www.empireranchfoundation.org>empire-ranch, retrieved Feb. 10, 2022.

18. John Boessenecker, op. cit. p. 74.

19. Pamela Potter, op. cit. p. 70.

20. "The Adams-Finley Murders," *Arizona Weekly Miner,* Oct. 4, 1878, p.2.

21. Larry D. Ball, op cit. p.113.

22. John Boessenecker, op. cit. p. 78.

23. "The Arizona Horror. Details of the Killing of Captain Adams and Mr. Finley," *The Pioneer,* Sat. Sept. 14, 1878.

24. "A Foul Murder," *San Jose Weekly Mercury,* Sept. 12, 1838.

25. Letter from Vicente Marischal to William H. Adams, Oct. 23, 1878, in Pamela Potter, op. cit.

26. *San Jose Weekly Mercury,* Dec. 26, 1878.

27. "The Honored Dead," *The Pioneer,* Dec. 28, 1878.

Epilogue

"No man or woman born, coward or brave, can shun his destiny."

–Homer, *The Iliad*

In the wake of the Adams-Finley murders, Guadalupe Celaya and the rest of his gang continued to pull off a series of highway robberies in Arizona and Sonora, Mexico. Wells Fargo & Co. enlisted another prominent California lawman named Bob Paul to hunt Celaya. Paul quickly captured gang member Joaquin Franco. The company also threatened to suspend operations in the territory. Somehow that got the attention of Governor Mariscal who ordered a detachment of border guards to round up the Celaya gang. In the sweep, the *Federales* captured or killed in shoot-outs several of the gang members including a pair who confessed to being part of the Davidson Canyon ambush. With Florentino Sais and Gregorio Acre still in the Magdalena jail, only Celaya remained at large. That ended on February 2, 1879, when soldiers cornered Celaya in a ravine at night. Before he could escape, the soldiers riddled the *bandido* with bullets. [1]

However, in the convulsed nature of the Mexican politics, Governor Marsical was overthrown, and the incarcerated members of the Celaya gang were released. Florentino Sais found a new gang association with the Cow-Boys, teaming up with an outlaw named Pete Spence. U.S. Marshal Crawley Dake, distraught and discouraged by the loss of two such able lawmen as Adams and Cornelius Finley only ten days after deputizing them, searched around for their replacements to help him stem the rising tide of violence. He focused on a band of brothers, recently removed from Dodge City, Kansas and other points west who were reuniting in Arizona along with their common-law wives. Their family name was Earp.

The Earp brothers-James, Virgil, Wyatt, Morgan and Warren – in aggregate offered some law enforcement experience, but none of them would pass a modern background check, given their previous arrest records and backgrounds as pimps, sporting men (gamblers), and even horse thieves. In a world where the border between law-abiding and law-breaking was very fluid, the Earps followed the money. In Arizona to try their luck in silver mining, the cash stipend of the deputy's job was enough inducement for them to sign on. Over the next few years, the Earps-particularly Wyatt- would become the most famous lawmen of the Old West.

It is not the purpose of this story to detail the saga of Wyatt Earp. The tensions and animosities that developed between the Earps and the Cow-Boys, particularly the faction headed by the Clanton clan, have been well-documented and told many times. The Clantons formed a working partnership with Cornelius Finley's cousins the Mclaurys, who had established ranches in the Babocomari Valley and Sulphur Springs Valley, each about twenty miles from where the boomtown of Tombstone would soon spring up. Tom and Frank McLaury would buy and sell cattle stolen in Mexico or Arizona by the Clantons. [2.] Used to having free rein for their various exploits, the Clantons and McLaurys resented the intrusion of the Earps into their affairs. The Earps had come to Arizona to make money. In addition to holding various law enforcement positions or riding shotgun guard for stage lines, they acquired interests in several mines, gambling houses and saloons. Wyatt Earp had his eye on the Cochise County sheriff's job. County sheriffs were also tax collectors and could pocket ten percent of their collections. In a mining boomtown like Tombstone that represented a small fortune. The Clantons supported the incumbent sheriff, Johnny Behan, who mostly looked the other way at their robberies and cattle thieving. The Earps, with authority in either local, county or federal jurisdictions, posed a threat, and their competing gambling houses cut into the Cow-Boys profits even more. It even got more personal. Wyatt Earp and Sheriff Behan both coveted the attention of the same woman, Josephine Marcus. After several run-ins, the situation escalated to drunken altercations, arrests and public death threats. Both sides had had had enough. What was to come was the most dramatic showdown in western history.

The climax, which has come to be known as the Gunfight at O.K. Corral, is the most researched, recounted and regurgitated half-minute in the story of the west. How Wyatt, Virgil, and Morgan Earp, along with their gunfighter friend Dr. John H. "Doc" Holliday walked down the street four abreast to confront five members of the Clanton gang in an empty lot adjacent to the O.K. Corral has been the subject of countless books, television and motion picture dramatizations, and Tombstone re-enactments. Historians and wild-west afficionados still debate what sparked the first shot, who shot whom, and whether it was frontier justice or grudge killing.

In any event, after 30 bullets in 30 seconds, two Earp brothers and Doc Holliday were wounded (In a career of gunfighting, Wyatt Earp was never wounded) and three of the Cow-Boys were killed, including Tom and Frank McLaury. The Earps and Holliday were arrested for murder. At the preliminary hearing, the prosecution team included another

McLaury brother and Finley relative, the vengeful attorney Will McLaury. The defense was headed by the famous California gold rush publisher and orator Tom Fitch. After a month-long hearing, the Earps were vindicated. The Clantons swore revenge. Seeking to kill the Earps, the Clanton gang stealthily ambushed Virgil Earp, permanently crippling his arm. They followed by killing Morgan Earp with a shotgun blast as he played billiards one evening. When justice for his brothers from the courts was not forthcoming, the switch on Wyatt Earp's internal control mechanism flipped, and he took the law into his own hands.

In what became called the "Vendetta Ride from Hell," Wyatt Earp, accompanied variously by younger brother Warren, Doc Holliday and such colorful characters as Texas Jack Vermillion, Turkey Creek Johnson, Harelip Charlie Smith and sometime-outlaw Sherman McMasters, systematically tracked, found and killed - some say executed - those he held responsible for his brothers' shootings. Cow-Boys Curly Bill Brocius, Frank Stilwell and John Ringo all died in set piece confrontations with the Earp deputies (although the latter may have been a suicide brought on by the Earp pursuit). At a coroner's inquest over the death of Morgan Earp, Marietta Spence, the wife of suspected outlaw Pete Spence, had implicated a "half-breed" Cow-Boy known as Indian Charley as having been an accomplice with her husband in the killing. Indian Charley was initially incorrectly identified as Florentino Cruz, but in fact was the same Florentino Sais who had murdered Deputy Marshals Adams and Finley three years earlier. On March 22, 1882, the Earp vendetta posse caught up with Sais at a woodcutting camp near South Pass of the Dragoon Mountains and as the former Celaya *bandido* ran, the deputies remorselessly avenged the deaths of Morgan Earp and of John Hicks Adams and Cornelius Finley. [3]

To avoid prosecution, the avenging angles of the vendetta left Arizona Territory for good. They had stained the reputation of the marshalcy and Marshal Crawley Dake was soon replaced.

Wyatt Earp, himself, wandered through the west and for a while even ran a saloon in Nome, during the Alaskan gold rush. He took Josephine Marcus as his fourth wife and eventually settled in Los Angeles. He spent his later years carefully recasting his life in an unpublished autobiography and in collaboration with a pliant biographer named Stuart Lake. He died in 1929 and is buried in Colma, California. His widow carefully sanitized his memoirs, removing references to the sporting life of brothels, laudanum and gambling, leaving the burnished legend of Wyatt Earp we have today.

* * *

John Sevenoaks, brother-in-law of Cornelius Finely, became superintendent of the San Pedro mine and owner of the Last Chance mine in Tombstone where he was acquainted with Wyatt Earp. After the Tombstone mines flooded, he relocated to San Diego and ran an icehouse. By the 1880s, miners had exhausted the best silver ores and most of the Arizona silver mines closed and most of the boom towns became ghost towns. Mining attention turned elsewhere to rich veins of copper.

A trio of Captain Adams's contemporary California lawmen deserve further mention. Nicholas R. Harris had succeeded Adams twice as Sheriff of Santa Clara County. He participated in several of the manhunts and was an esteemed bandit hunter in his own right. He followed his sheriff's position by becoming a U.S. Secret Service Agent in 1882. Harris dropped dead on the streets of San Francisco in 1902.

Captain Adams's arch-rival for apex lawman, Alameda County Sheriff Harry N. Morse, later founded the Harry N. Morse Detective Agency of California. Noted for gun duels with Hispanic *bandidos,* Morse had captured the nephew of Joaquin Murrieta and had been instrumental in ultimately locating Tiburcio Vasquez in 1874. His greatest accomplishment may have been the apprehension of Charles E. Boles, otherwise known as Black Bart. Black Bart became California's most wanted stage robber in the 1880s. Together with associate James Hume (see following) and utilizing modern for the times detective work, Morse tracked down the gentleman highwayman and extracted a confession. He worked well into the 20th century and died in 1912.

James B. Hume had been Under Sheriff of El Dorado County at the time of the Bullion Bend stage robbery. Hume had found the body of his friend Joseph Staples and the gravely wounded George Ranney at the Somerset House and had taken the captured Tom Poole back to Placerville. He was, coincidentally, another very distant relative of Cornelius Finley and the McLaurys, the grandson of their great granduncle. He later served as deputy warden of Nevada State Prison and as a detective for Wells Fargo & Co. After Black Bart dropped a handkerchief at the scene of a stage robbery, Hume doggedly visited every laundry in San Francisco until finding one that could identify the laundry mark. Hume also pioneered the art of criminal profiling and studied ballistics, foreshadowing the fictional Sherlock Holmes (first appearing in 1887) and more modern real-life detective work. He never retired and died in Berkeley, California in 1904.

Charles Boles borrowed the pseudonym Black Bart from a character in a small, serialized pulp story called *"The Case of Summerfield"* by William Henry Rhodes, published in 1871. That fictional character was closely modeled after Captain

Rufus Henry Ingram of the Bullion Bend robberies. The author described his character as having "served in the late civil war under [General Sterling] Price and Quantrell, [sic] with the Confederate army" and much of the action takes place in the gold country, including at a railroad curve above Auburn – an obvious allusion to Bullion Bend. Further, the character also disappears without a trace. Why the real-life gentleman stage robber Boles/Black Bart would model his criminal persona after a literary character, much less after the real enigmatic Captain Ingram, is fascinating to ponder[4]

As for the other lawmen in the Bullion Bend robbery, George Ranney miraculously recovered from his multiple wounds and worked as a millwright until hallucinations about his experience affected his mind. He died in the California Mental Facility at Stockton in 1912. Deputy J.D. Van Eaton left law enforcement, moved to San Jose and died in 1884.

Among the notorious *bandidos* left unaccounted was Clodovio Chavez of the Vasquez gang who threatened to kill anyone involved in the prosecution of Tiburcio Vasquez. From jail awaiting execution, Vasquez published a message to Chavez advising him to drop such threats and plans in order to avoid facing the gallows himself. Chavez heeded the words of his *jefe* (leader) and removed to Arizona, finding work as a ranch hand on Baker's Rancho. When a former Californian recognized Chavez, he informed others. A man named C.S. Calvig sought out Chavez, knowing there was a reward on his head, dead or alive. Confronted, Chavez turned to run and Calvig dispatched the last of the Tres Pinos *bandidos* with a shotgun load through his back. [5]

According to an oral history passed down, many years after the execution of Tiburcio Vasquez, a worker at the county jail took home some lumber from a wood pile at the jail to build his wife a new wash line. Alerted to the fact that the lumber came from the Vasquez gallows, the man's wife made him burn it down.

At the time of this writing, the current Santa Clara County Sheriff, the first woman statewide to hold that position, recently announced her retirement after twenty years in office. The times, they are a changin'.

* * *

The North American continent plays such an important role in our story. Much of it has been altered by what humans have placed upon its surface or dug from it over the last couple of centuries. Highways connect cities. Farmland replaces open space and housing tracts replace the farmland. Dams control the flow of rivers. Pollution alters the air, water and land and dramatic climate change threatens it all. Human endeavor has created wealth, prosperity and progress unknown in the 19th century, but not without a price.

By far, the greatest sacrifice has been borne by the indigenous native peoples who lost their ancestral lands on the plains, the pueblos of the southwest or in the valleys of California. These original Americans lost their traditional ways of life, their sources of food such as the buffalo, and saw the suppression of their cultures and religions. Forced into resettlement, many even lost their lives in great number from disease, neglect and even official genocidal public policies. Other long-established groups also continued to be deprived of opportunities and full equality. The descendants of *Californios* still face discrimination long after the collapse of the *ranchos* and the mission system. Descendants of African American slaves struggle daily for equal rights under the law a century and a half after the Civil War. More recent immigrants from the Americas, Asia and elsewhere still struggle as they choose to assimilate, integrate or stay separate from the dominant population.

All the change since the days of John Hicks Adams would bewilder him, while some things would remain familiar. St. Louis celebrates being the Gateway to the West with a great Arch. The Mississippi still drains the continent into the Gulf of Mexico, passing through New Orleans, the most Spanish,

French, Southern, African American, Caribbean and just plain American city, on its way to the Gulf of Mexico. Santa Fe, New Mexico now offers a lively artists' colony to visitors. Interstate Highway 80 runs pretty much parallel to the old California-Oregon Trail; some wagon ruts are still visible. The geographic landmarks such as Chimney Rock or Independence Rock sill mark the way. Modern travelers can cross the prairies and mountains in air-conditioned comfort in a matter of days instead of four to six months in a wagon. (This author, in his mis-spent youth once team drove I-80 from Illinois to San Jose in 36 hours, including a short nap in Wyoming waiting for a gas station to open.). Of course, with air travel, a person can skip the continent altogether and fly coast to coast in less than half a day. Tombstone faded from boom to bust when the local mines flooded in the 1880s, but still celebrates its notorious past with daily gunfighter reenactments for the tourists. The deserts of the great western basin are still uninviting but all-weather highways now allow access over the Sierra Nevada passes year-round.

On the western side of the Sierra range, California opens as one of the world's top half-dozen economies, fueled by agriculture, entertainment, tourism and technology. The Sierra and Lake Tahoe attract vacationers, backpackers and winter sports enthusiasts year-round. The great valleys provide more than half the nation's fruit, vegetables, nuts, rice and wine. Day trippers along State Route 49 enjoy many of the former gold country towns like Placerville or Georgetown, offering restored gold rush buildings, interesting museums, and cozy bed and breakfast inns. School kids can still try mining for gold in the American River, although the real mines are long closed. The once sleepy pueblo-turned entertainment mecca of Los Angeles now sprawls across hundreds of square miles of housing and asphalt freeways. It is the second largest Mexican city in the world and Hispanics are now the demographic majority in the state. Some say Mexico is slowly reclaiming what it lost with the Treaty of Guadalupe Hidalgo. Many of the original Spanish missions are still active parish churches, although several are in various states of disrepair. Several thousand native California Indians lie in unmarked graves on the mission grounds at San Juan Bautista and the other missions. The old Mexican capital of Monterey became a booming sardine fishing port, captured in the novels of John Steinbeck, and now peacefully attracts tourists to a world-class aquarium. San Francisco rebuilt itself after a devastating fire and earthquake in 1906 to become the financial center of the west, troop embarkation port during World War II, epicenter of the drugs/sex/rock-n-roll 1960s and remains a major international tourist destination. After decades in the shadow of San Francisco, San Jose emerged as the unofficial capital of "Silicon Valley" and the country's tenth largest city. The Santa Clara Valley has traded most of its orchards for housing and high technology campuses, including the headquarters for some of the world's most capitalized companies like Apple and Meta. The quicksilver mines finally closed half a century ago. In Gilroy, the "Garlic Capital of the World," the local council recently erected a mission bell, a replica of those that once lined El Camino Real from south to north, despite the protest of the few remaining members of the Amah Mutsun tribe.

* * *

Matilda Jane Pomeroy Adams recovered from the shock of her husband's murder and regained her health, living in the Willow Glen area of San Jose until her death in 1901. She is buried near her husband in Oak Hills Memorial Cemetery in San Jose. Of the Adams children, most remained in Santa Clara County. Sarah Jane had married James Reed, youngest survivor of the ill-fated Donner Party. The Reeds were a prominent family in early San Jose. She died in 1891. William Humboldt, who had served as his father's deputy sheriff from 1873 to 1876, married Nellie Ackley and became a rancher and French prune orchardist in the Llagas District west of the current city of Morgan Hill. He died following a wagon accident in 1923.

Nellie Melissa married Frank E. Stark and remained in San Jose, dying in 1925. Eldest daughter Mary Hannah married James Ross Hanna and moved to Alameda County, where she died in Livermore in 1930. Alice Melissa, widow of jailer W.H. Hendrick. who was killed in the jail break, years later was married to John W. Gordon. She died in San Francisco in 1933. Charles Clinton volunteered during the Spanish American War, serving in Co. L, 7th California Infantry. A single man, he was listed as a cannery worker in the 1930 U.S Census and he lived with brother William on the Llagas ranch. Abraham Lincoln married Florence Edith Brendon. He was a self-employed trucker in southern California in the 1930 Census records before dying in Los Angeles in 1938.

The Adams's descendants, now in the fourth, fifth and sixth generations, have dispersed throughout the state and beyond, although many still reside in Santa Clara County. Several generations have grown up on the Adams Ranch between Morgan Hill and New Almaden and still live and work on part of the original property today. In 1995, reflecting on his great grandfather, William Harry "Bill" Adams, said "Those were wild and wooly times and he [Captain Adams] was a wild and wooly guy."[6] A badass, indeed.

* * *

225

What then of the legacy of Sheriff John Hicks Adams? His surname appears on a few streets and he shares it with the Amah Mutsun native Americans at the donated school site called Chitactac - Adams. For a time, a meeting space was named for him in the Santa Clara County Sheriff's Department. The U.S. Justice Department – U. S. Marshals Office recognizes both Adams and Cornelius Finley as heroes who died in the line of duty. Serious western scholars and self-described *cowboy nerds* have heard of his gunfight with the Confederate partisans or his hanging of Tiburcio Vasquez. His family continue to refer to him as *Captain Jack.*

Among the greater public, however, his reputation doesn't extend so far. He never achieved the notoriety or fame of a Wild Bill Hickok or Bat Masterson. And even those household names pale when the subject becomes Wyatt Earp. Some heroes of the west achieved much of their legacy by the way they died, as well as how they lived: Crockett at the Alamo; Custer at the Little Big Horn (both of those deaths have become controversial); or Hickok holding the card hand of aces and eights in a Deadwood saloon. Abraham Lincoln, almost certainly our greatest president, nevertheless transcended mortality with his martyr's death. My generation still wonders how much more John F. Kennedy, his brother Robert, or Martin Luther King would have accomplished had they not been assassinated. Even villains get a status bump in death: Jesse James betrayed and shot from behind by cowardly Robert Ford; Billy the Kid hunted and killed by former associate Pat Garrett; or Butch Cassidy and the Sundance Kid going out in a blaze of military gunfire (perhaps) in Bolivia. The gruesome death of Adams and Finley may have briefly made the headlines but seems to have had little lasting impact.

Some historical characters, whether politicians or *pistoleros,* seemed highly aware of their own reputations in their own lifetimes. Would Hickok be as interesting without the fancy wardrobe or exquisite pair of Navy pistols in his gun belt, handles facing for a quick cross-draw? William F. "Buffalo Bill" Cody may have been the premier buffalo hunter of his era, but he achieved near immortality only after years of self-promotion with his world-touring Wild West Show. John F. Fremont was the most intrepid explorer-geographer of his day but relied on political connections and well-edited (by his literary wife) book sales to propel his career forward and assure his place in history. More self-effacing heroes often found themselves disregarded. It took financial necessity for Ulysses S. Grant to even write his memoirs with the help of Mark Twain, and it took a century before Grant was fully appreciated not only as the general who won the Civil War but as an able and good president during Reconstruction. As Sheriff, John

Hicks Adams was superbly competent and accomplished, but as a politician he seemed satisfied to let his record speak for itself. In five elections that seemed sufficient, but when the times changed and the support of his political party ebbed away, reputation alone proved not enough.

Another factor in how historical figures fare when remembered is their attachment to an ideology. Sometimes the ideology is embraced by the figure in life and sometimes the figure is appropriated by a cause later. John Brown was a homicidal fanatic, but he was sanctified as a martyr to the abolitionist cause. Lincoln himself effected emancipation of the slaves primarily to save the Union, but he became Father Abraham to millions of freed African Americans. How Confederate figures are remembered today depends on one's view of "the Cause," even as statues topple in public parks across the south. In our times, in California, Cesar Chavez and Dolores Huerta fought with dignity for the rights of Mexican America farmworkers. But how does one justify naming schools or health facilities after Tiburcio Vasquez, who terrorized *Californio* and Anglo citizens with equal viciousness? Yet, Vasquez is seen in some circles as a hero even today. In the human consciousness, one person's terrorist is another's freedom fighter. Captain Adams was a life-long Republican and public servant. But he was not a crusader. His job was to follow orders and he expected others to follow his orders. He sought to keep the peace, administer justice and follow the laws of the land. Those are admirable qualities indeed, but they don't create headlines or lasting images.

Captain Adams was certainly a brave man. Many times, he faced down an adversary without blinking. His iconic stand in front of the partisan rangers, where he took a pistol ball to the chest that should have killed him but recovered when it glanced off his pocket watch and he returned fire to fell his assailant is worthy of Hollywood. And Adams was steadfast. Sheriffs throughout the state knew they could count on his cooperation and help. Had Adams been paid by hours in the saddle or by miles logged in dogged pursuit of thieves and killers, he would have earned more than he ever did in the mines. By all measures, he proved heroic.

When J.H. Adams retired briefly in 1870, the *San Jose Daily Mercury* offered this assessment of the outgoing sheriff: "No more faithful or competent officer in the special line of his duties has this state ever had. His bravery in making desperate arrests only equaled by his unassuming modesty. His kindness of heart and humane consideration for those brought under the ban of the law have characterized his whole official course." [7]

Yet from the time of the ancient Greek tragedies, people seem to prefer the anti-hero. Something about the person of potential greatness being brought low by a character flaw resonates in the popular mind. Overcoming great odds despite such a flaw elevates a hero to demi-god status. Wyatt Earp possessed all the characteristics of a great frontier lawman: extreme bravery, determination, gunfighting skill and a sense of righteousness. But his checkered past and vengeful second nature made him more complex and ultimately more compelling a figure. If Wyatt Earp was the anti-hero, John Hicks Adams was the anti-Earp. Nothing in the historical record suggests he harbored strong compulsions like gambling or drink. He worked for his pay as a public servant in a position most shied away from. He was more modest than boastful. On those occasions he was absent from his wife and family, he returned – except from his last fatal trip– to take care of business at home. He was not a transitional figure in the evolution of law enforcement. He was a sheriff and deputy marshal of the old school. But he helped transition a lawless California into a more modern, just society. He is revered by his descendants and admired by those who know his story. More should. And that will be enough.

The End

Notes:

1. John Boessenecker, *Ride the Devil's Herd. Wyatt Earp's Epic Battle Against the West's Biggest Outlaw Gang*, Toronto: The Hanover Press, 2021, pp. 76-78.

2. Ibid. pp. 84-85.

3. Larry D. Ball, *The United States Marshals of New Mexico and Arizona territories, 1846–1912*, Albuquerque: University of New Mexico Press, 1940, pp. 120-127.

4. J.G. Kearney, *Not of the Ruling Power. Captain Ingram's Partisan Rangers in California*, Bloomington IN: Xlibris (self published) 2016.

5. Sitemap True Crime Blog, https://www.historicalcrimedetective.com/content/, retrieved Feb. 14, 2022.

6. William H. "Bill" Adams, video presentation, Morgan Hill Historical Society, April 26, 1995.

7. *San Jose Daily Mercury*, May 8, 1870.

Acknowledgements

Journalists strive to shield their sources. However, the many people who contributed to this work of historical journalism deserve recognition and gratitude.

Special thanks to dear friend Cathy Castillo, a superb journalist and editor in her own right, and my second pair of eyes. In addition, the memory of her late husband, *mi compadre* Elias Castillio, served as an inspiration for me to tackle this project at this later stage of my career.

Local historian, writer and wine aficionado Mike Monroe was in many ways the catalyst for launching this book. *A su salud!*

There is a special place in Paradise for research librarians, history museum curators and historical society docents. I owe a debt of gratitude to many: Shane Curtin and Mike Lara at the California Room, Martin Luther King Library, City of San Jose /San Jose State University; Rubie Bajwa-Dulay, Senior Management Analyst and Archivist, Santa Clara County Archives/ Clerk-Recorder's Office, County of Santa Clara; Mary Z. Rose, Archival Research Manager,

Madison County (Illinois) Historical Society; Lynda Will, Parks Program Coordinator Parks and Recreation Department, County of Santa Clara; Susan Voss, Manager-Gilroy Historical Museum, City of Gilroy; Mary Cory, El Dorado County Historical Museum, El Dorado County Historical Society; Kathy Devine, Museum Director and Kathy Sullivan, my past co-president, Morgan Hill Historical Society; Janene Crawford. Researcher, Santa Clara County Historical and Genealogical Society; Charlene Duval and Leilani Marshall, Sourisseau Academy for State and Local History, San Jose State University; Cate Mills, Curator of Library, Archives and Multimedia, History San Jose.

Special kudos to retired Santa Clara County Deputy Sheriff Rick Sprain, who as departmental historian, gathered and preserved boxes of material about historical Santa Clara County sheriffs and has made the material available at the County Archives.

This author enjoyed enthusiastic encouragement and access from descendants of John Hicks Adams: Loreen (Mrs. William) Adams, Wally Adams, Sean Adams, Sallie Jensen - all of the Llagas Ranch, Morgan Hill, California, and Rebecca Adams Pasquinelli of Monte Sereno, California (by coincidence, a former student of the author); Johny Adams of Gilroy, California; Randy (Mrs. Robert) Adams of Rochester,

234

Minnesota. All generously contributed. Additional material was provided by Garey and Cheryle Cearlock of Bend, Oregon.

Thanks also to fellow academic with similar research interests, Loftin "Woody" Woodiel, Ph.D., Associate Professor of Criminal Justice at Missouri Baptist University for his encouragement and generous Foreword. And to good friends who always encouraged me: Tim Hendrick, Robert Izmirian, Jeff Longshaw and Gail Love, Richard Anderson and cousin Christy Johansen. I also deeply appreciate the encouragement and advice of Brad Jones and Cinda Meister at BookSmart, Morgan Hill.

Transition from manuscript to print and digital reality could not have been possible without the talent and effort of designer Briana Carlson Monaco and the patience and professionalism of Emily Veeh and the folks at Bookstand Publishing. Many thanks.

Most importantly, eternal gratitude and love to my wife Kathie, who endured many lonely hours as a writer's spouse and who, along with our daughters Christina and Alysia, their husbands Brian and G.O., and our grandchildren Owen, Will and Emma, inspires me daily.

Selected Bibliography

Books

Ambrose, Stephen E., *Undaunted Courage. Meriwether Lewis, Thomas Jefferson and Opening the American West,* New York: Touchstone-Simon & Shuster, 1996.

Arbuckle, Clyde, *History of San Jose,* San Jose: Memorabilia of San Jose, 1986.

Ball, Larry D., *The United States Marshals of New Mexico and Arizona Territories 1846–1912,* Albuquerque: University of New Mexico Press, 1978.

Beilharz, Edwin A. and DeMers Donald O. Jr., *San Jose. California's First City,* Tulsa, OK: Continental Heritage Press, 1980.

Boessenecker, John, *Badge and Buckshot. Lawlessness in Old California,* Norman: University of Oklahoma Press, 1988.

_____. *Bandido. The Life and Times of Tiburcio Vasquez,* Norman: University of Oklahoma Press, 2010.

_____, *Ride the Devil's Herd. Wyatt Earp's Epic Battle Against the West's Biggest Outlaw Gang.* Toronto: Hanover Square Press, 2020.

Castillo, Elias, *A Cross of Thorns. The Enslavement of California's Indians by the Spanish Missions,* Fresno: Craven Street Books, 2015.

Clavin, Tom, *Tombstone. The Earp Brothers, Doc Holliday and the Vendetta Ride from Hell,* New York: St. Martin's Press, 2020.

Dickson, Samuel, *Tales of San Francisco*, Stanford, CA: Stanford University Press, 1960.

DiSalvo, Chris, *San Jose &. Silicon Valley. Primed for the 21st Century*, Montgomery, AL: Community Communications Inc., 1997.

Fernando-Armesto, Felipe, *Our America. A Hispanic History of the United States*, New York: W.W. Norton & Co., 2014.

Guinn, J.M., *History of the State of California & Bibliographical Record of Coast Counties, California*, Chicago: The Chapman Publishing Co., 1904.

Hannah-Jones, Nikole et al., *The 1619 Project–A New Origin Story*, New York: One World Books, 2021.

Harte, Bret, *Tales of the West*, New York: Avenel Books, 1991.

Kearney, J.G., *Not of the Ruling Power. Captain Ingram's Partisan Rangers in California*, Bloomington IN: Xlibris, 2016.

Meldahl, Keith Heyer, *Hard Road West. History and Geology along the Gold Rush Trail*, Chicago: University of Chicago Press, 2008.

Merry, Robert W., *A Country of Vast Designs. James K. Polk, the Mexican War and the Conquest of the American Continent*, New York: Simon & Shuster, 2009.

Mora-Torres, Gregorio (ed. and trans.), *Californio Voices. The Oral Memoirs of Jose Maria Amador and Lorenzo Asisara*, Denton, TX: University of North Texas Press, 2005.

Peck J.M., *Guide for Emigrants, containing sketches of Illinois, Missouri and the Adjacent Parts*, Boston: Lincoln & Edwards, 1831.

Pen Pictures from the Garden of the World or Santa Clara County, California, H.S. Foote (ed), Chicago: The Lewis Publishing Co., 1888.

Sawyer, Eugene T., *History of Santa Clara County, California,* Historic Record Co., 1922.

Tucker, Phillip Thomas, *Exodus from the Alamo,* Philadelphia: Casemate Publishers, 2010.

Winchester, Simon, *Land,* New York: Harper Perennial, 2022.

Yadon, Laurence J., and Anderson, Dan, *Arizona Gunfighters,* Gretna LA: Pelican Publishing Co., 2010.

Articles and Digital Sources

"A Brief History of Gilroy," City of Gilroy, CA, https://www.cityofgilroy.org>History-of-Gilroy.

"African-Americans in the Mississippi River Valley 1857–1900, Northern Illinois Press, https://digital.lib.niu.edu>twain>liberty.

"Alton and the Mississippi River," *MCHS News,* Madison County Historical Society, Vol. 12, No. 5, September 2014, https://madcohistory.org>uploads.

Antonucci, David C., "Yours, Mine, Ours. An Explanative History of the People and Environment of Lake Tahoe," https://www.tahoefact.com>Yours-Mine-Ours-v10-e.

Barker, Eugene C. and Pohil, James W., "Texas Revolution," *Handbook of Texas*, Texas State Historical Association, https://www.tshaonline.org>handbook>entries>texas.

Beilharz, Alan, "Legacy of the California Gold Rush," *Discover Coloma: A Teacher's Guide,* Gold Discovery Park Association, https://www.marshallgold.com/.

"California Civil War History," American Civil War Homepage, http://www.thomaslegion.net>americancivilwar.>calif.

"California's Role in the Civil War," *The Cannon's Mouth,* California Historical Artillery Society, October 2016.

"Capt John Hicks Adams," https://www.findagrave.com/memorial/12500188/john-hicks-adams.

"Causes of Texas Independence," https://www.exlors.com>summary>causes-ofTexasIndependence.

Cole, David, "Survey of U.S. Army Uniforms, Weapons and Accoutrements," from J. and S.G. Gideon, *General Regulations for the Army 1847,* Washington, D.C. 1847, https//history.army.mil>uniforms>survey.

Correa, Tom, "John Hicks Adams – One of America's Great Old West Lawmen," *American Cowboy Chronicle,* June 5, 2015.

"Crossing at St. Joseph," Oregon-California Trails Association, https://www.gatewqay-octa.org>trail-history.

DeLay, Brian, "It's Time to Remember the Role of Indians in the Mexican American War," History News Network, https://historynewsnetwork.org>article.

"Donner and Reed Wagon Train Incident," National Park Service, https://www.nps.gov>cali>learn>historyculture.

"Drytown, Cal.," https://www.cali49.com>hwy49>drytown-cal.

Dutka, Barry L., "New York Discovers Gold! In California," *California History,* University of California Press, Vol. 63, No. 4 (fall 1984).

"Elijah Parrish Lovejoy," https://nationalabolitionhalloffameandmuseum.org.

"Four Foot Soldiers on the Trail – An Illinois Odyssey," https://www.santafetrailresearch.com>research>fourfootsoldio ersonthetrail.

Gittings, Rowland R., "Abraham Lincoln Once Declined the Governorship of Oregon," *The Oregon Sunday Journal*, Feb. 11, 1912, http://www.ochcom.org>pdf>Lincoln-OR-Gov.

Hart, Richard E., "Pedro Pino: Governor of Zuni Pueblo, 1830–1878," University Press of Colorado, 2003, https://www.jstor.org>stable.

"History of Illinois," https://www.history.com>topicas>us-states>Illinois.

"History of Edwardsville," https://townsquarepublications.com/regions/midwest/Illinois/E dwardsville.

"John Hicks Adams," *The History Junkie*, 2021, https://thehistoryjunkie.com>john-hicks-adams-biography.

Kemble, John Haskell, "The Panama Route to the Pacific Coast, 1848-1869," *Pacific Historical Review*, Vol. 7, No. 1, University of California Press, 1938, https://doi.org/10.2037/3633844.

"Lamp Oil from Castor Beans," *Illinois Historical Anecdotes*, Chicago, 1940, http://genealogytrails.com>ill>illinois.

Lenon, Robert, "The Patagonia Area Mining Districts, Santa Cruz County Arizona 1539–1930," 1998, https://www.miningfoundationsssw.org,

Lummis, Charles F., "Pioneer Transportation in America," *McClure's Magazine*, Vol. xxvi, p. 83, in Hartman, William Amos, "The California and Oregon Trail, 1849-1860," *The*

Quarterly of the Oregon Historical Society, Vol. XXV, No. 1, March 1924, http://www.jstor.org/stable/20610264.

Mero, William, "Joaquin Murrieta: Literary Fiction or Historical Fact?," https://www.cocohistory.org>essays-murrieta.

"Miller v. Dale 92 U.S. 473 (1875)," https://supreme.justia.com>cases>federal.

Myers, Lee, "Illinois Volunteers in New Mexico 1847–1848," New Mexico Historical Review, 47, 1, 2021, https://digitalrepository.unm.edu/nmhr/vol47/iss1/2.

"Old Courthouse History," The Superior Court of California, County of Santa Clara, https://www.scscourt.org>community>och-history.

"Old Hangtown," *The Gold Rush Chronicles,* http://goldrushchronicles.com>hangtown.

"Pacific Mail Steamship Company," https://www.foundsf.org.title=Pacific.

Patel, Vinay R, "Castor Oil: Properties, Uses, and Optimization of Processing Parameters in Commercial Production," https://www.nebi.nim.nih.gov>articles (PMC 5015816).

Potter, Pamela, "A well-known lawman from California and a relative of the McLaurys were shot down in Arizona Territory," *Wild West,* August 2003.

Ransome, Frederick Leslie, "Notes on Some Mining Districts in Humboldt County Nevada," Washington D.C.: Department of the Interior, *U.S. Geological Survey Bulletin* 414, 1909.

Reader, Phil, "Copperheads, Sesesh Men and Confederate Guerilas: Pro-Confederate Activities in Santa Cruz County during the Civil War," *Local History*, Santa Cruz Public Libraries, https://www.historysantacruzpl.org>files>original.

242

_____, "Charole: The Life of Branciforte Bandido Faustino Lorenzana," Local History-Santa Cruz Public Libraries, https://history.santacruzpl.org/omeka.

"Shurtleff College," https://www.lostcolleges.com>Shurtleff-College.

Sitemap "True Crime Blog," https://www.historicalcrimedetective.com/content/.

Stauffer, Alvin P., "The Quartermaster's Department and the Mexican War," *Quartermaster Review*, U.S. Army Quartermaster Foundation, May-June 1950, http://old.quartermasterfoundation.org>quartermaster.

"St. Joseph, Missouri – Jumping Off To The West," *Legends of the West*, https://www.legendsofamerica.com>mo-stjoseph.

"The Early History of Edwardsville and Leclaire," https://www.madison.Illinoisgenweb.org>town-histories>.

"The Mexican War," *Digital History*, https://www.digitalhistory.uh.edu>disp-textbook.

"The Panama Route," University of California Press, https://publishing.cdlib.org>ucpressbooks>vbiew.

"Vail, Hislop and Harvey 1877-1878," Empire Ranch Foundation, https://www.empireranchfoundation.org>empire-ranch.

Vande Creek, Drew, "The Mexican American War," http://digital.lib.niu.edu/islandora/object/niu-lincoln%3A32025.

Wyman, Walker D., "The Military Phase of Santa Fe Freighting, 1846-1865," *Kansas Historical Journal*, Vol. 1, No. 5, November 1932.

Newspapers

"Many Old Houses Still Remain," *Edwardsville Intelligencer*, Centennial Edition, 1912.

"Old Landmark Going," *Edwardsville Intelligencer*, Feb. 24, 1921.

Edwardsville Madison County Courier, Feb. 15, 1866, p. 3.

Alton Telegraph, November 1841.

"Remains of Captain Franklin Niles Laid to Rest," *Alton Telegraph*, Oct. 15, 1847.

Alton Telegraph, June 22, 1849, p. 4.

"Capt. John H. Adams, a Mexican Veteran and a 49-er – An Adventurous Life," *San Jose Pioneer Press*, 1878.

"The True Story of Hangtown," *Sacramento Daily Union*, col. 11, No. 55, April 24, 1889.

"Terrible Tragedy," *San Jose Mercury*, Feb. 15, 1866.

San Jose Daily Mercury, April 22, 1875.

San Jose Weekly Mercury, Aug. 14, 1873.

"South Almaden Quicksilver Mines," *San Jose Weekly Mercury*, June 1, 1876.

"South Almaden," *San Jose Weekly Mercury*, Nov. 2, 1876.

"South Almaden Mine," *San Jose Weekly Mercury*, May 10, 1877.

The Pioneer, June 16, 1877.

"The Arizona Horror. Details of the Killing of Captain Adams and Mr. Finley," *The Pioneer*, Sept. 14, 1878.

"The Adams-Finley Murders," *Arizona Weekly Miner*, Oct. 4, 1878, p. 2.

"A Foul Murder," *San Jose Weekly Mercury,* Sept. 12, 1878.

San Jose Weekly Mercury, Dec. 26, 1878.

"The Honored Dead," *The Pioneer,* Dec. 28, 1878.

San Jose Daily Mercury, May 8, 1870.

Journals, Diaries and Letters

John Quincy Adams, Journal, transcribed by Magnus R. Milnor, June 1988.

John Hicks Adams, Pocket Journal, July 21, 1874.

_____, Pocket Diary and Account Book, March 19, 1875.

_____, Pocket Diary and Account Book, March 19, 1878.

_____, Pocket Diary and Account Book, July 24, 1878.

Lincoln's Springfield: Letters from California and Oregon (1845-52), Spring Creek Series, Richard E. Hart ed., Springfield, IL, 2020.

Letter from Vicente Marischal to William H. Adams, Oct. 23, 1878.

David Wooster, letter, The Gold Rush: letters of David Wooster from California to the *Adrian, Michigan Expositor* 1850-1855, John Cumming ed. Mount Pleasant MI: The Cumming Press, 1972.

Fluery F. Keith, Diary, Aug. 18, 1850, in Landon, Michael N., "Chasing a Golden Dream: The Story of the California Trail," http://overlandtrails.lib.byu.edu>essay-ctrail

Genealogies

Descendants of Harry Eaton,"
http://www.djs.org.eatongenealogyreport.

History and Genealogy of the Pomeroy Family and collateral Lines-England-Ireland-America comprising the Ancestors and Descendants of George Pomeroy of Pennsylvania, William McL. And Nevin Pomeroy pub., 1958.

Jessie Evelyn Springer, Charles Springer of Cranehook-on-the-Delaware: His descendants and allied families, Edwardsville: Sept. 28, 1959.

John Culligan, McClaughry/McLaury and Allied Families, Delaware County NY Genealogical and History Site, https://www.dcnyhistoiry.org.familymclaughry, Feb. 3, 2022.

www.ancestry.comn and www.familysearch.com for the following:

- John Q. Adams
- Hannah Anne Hicks Adams
- John Adams (U.S. President)
- John Hicks Adams
- Matilda Jane Pomeroy Adams
- Mary Hannah Adams Hanna
- Alice Melissa Adams Hendricks Gordon
- Sarah Jane Adams Reed
- William Humboldt Adams
- Charles Clinton Adams
- Nellie M. Adams Stark
- Abraham Lincoln Adams
- Cornelius Finley
- James B. Hume
- Tom McLaury
- Frank McLaury

Miscellaneous

Almaden Quicksilver County Park Historic Trail, brochure, Santa Clara County Parks.

John Hicks Adams, Deed of Conveyance, April 4, 1849, Madison County Historical Society.

Chitactac-Adams Heritage Park, plaque, Mountain Charlie Chapter No. 1850, E Clampus Vitus, dedicated June 12, 1993.

Miller-Vasquez exhibit, Gilroy Historical Museum, Gilroy CA.

Johnston, Stewart, *Map of the Oregon Trail and Route to the California Gold Rush along the Humboldt River*, map 1893 in https://texashistory.unt.edu/ark/67531/metaph1933547/m1/1:ArlingtonLibrary, Nov.30 2021.

William H. Adams, video presentation, Morgan Hill Historical Society, April 26, 1995.

Personal Interviews and Correspondence

Mary Z. Rose, Madison County Historical Society, Edwardsville, IL.

Mary Cory, El Dorado County Historical Museum, Placerville, CA.

Lynda Will, Parks Program Coordinator, County of Santa Clara, CA.

Susan Voss, Director Gilroy Historical Museum, City of Gilroy, CA.

Janene Crawford, Santa Clara County Historical and Genealogical Society, CA.

Danny Michael, Winchester Rifle Museum, Cody, WY.

Descendants of John Hicks Adams:

- Loreen (Mrs. William) Adams
- Rebecca Adams Pasquinelli
- Wally Adams
- Sean Adams
- Sallie Jensen
- Johny Adams
- Randy (Mrs. Robert) Adams
- Cheryle and Garey Cearlock

Zorro (?).